NOH

NOH
The Classical Theater

by Yasuo Nakamura

translated by Don Kenny

with an introduction by
Earle Ernst

A WEATHERHILL BOOK

WALKER/WEATHERHILL, *New York & Tokyo*
IN COLLABORATION WITH TANKOSHA, KYOTO

This book was originally published in Japanese
by Tankosha, Kyoto, under the title *Noh*.

FIRST EDITION, 1971

Jointly published by John Weatherhill, Inc., of New York and Tokyo, and Tankosha
of Kyoto / Distributed in the Far East by JOHN WEATHERHILL, INC., 7-6-13 Roppongi,
Minato-ku, Tokyo 106, and in the United States by WALKER AND COMPANY, 720
Fifth Avenue, New York, N.Y. 10019 / Copyright © 1967, 1971, by Tankosha.
Printed in Japan

LCC CARD No. 77-98335
ISBN 0-8027-2439-6

Table of Contents

vi   *Contents*

NOH

The Noh: An Appreciation

by Earle Ernst

THE FIRST I SAW of Japan was Fuji rising imperceptibly from the edge of the sea, a last red patch of sunset behind it.

Outside Tokyo our plane came down in darkness. I waited around in the rain for an hour. A truck came along, stopped, I climbed in, and we drove toward the center of the ruined city through black, empty streets. The billet I was assigned to was all lit up; there were warm radiators, a well-stocked bar. After I got bourbon, I noticed eight or so soggy-looking Japanese men, who had come in from the street, setting up music stands at the other end of the room, taking instruments from battered cases. Then they began to play and sing: "Caledonia, Caledonia, what makes your big head so hard?" They sounded exactly like Woody Herman.

It had been a tiring day, Hawaii to Kwajalein to Guam to Japan, and to find this shocking performance at the end of it was intolerable. How could they play American jazz this way when it had been forbidden throughout the war? How could defeated men produce such a joyful sound? What sort of people were they?

The next morning (this was Friday, November 16, 1945) I went with my army orders to the sixth floor of Radio Tokyo, where I saw the officer in charge of the Civil Censorship Detach-

3

ment. I learned that in the interests of combating nationalist tendencies in Japanese society and strengthening those that were democratic (the Japanese had accepted the provisions of the Potsdam Declaration), all forms of communication were being censored—mail, radio, books, phonograph records, films, even the scripts of itinerant storytellers who performed in the streets for children, illustrating their tales with a series of drawings. My job, it turned out, was to see that nothing feudalistic or otherwise undemocratic went on in the postwar theater.

At a rough estimate, some seven hundred theatrical troupes were producing all sorts of plays, ranging, chronologically, from six-century-old Noh plays to the one, written yesterday, about the pitiable ex-soldier returning from Malaya to find his wife, who had thought him dead, remarried. The troupes came in all sizes and talents, from the poor players who toured country villages to the elite actors of Kabuki in the metropolises of Tokyo and Osaka.

The variety of productions was stunning. What looked very much like a Radio City show with acres of costumes, swiftly changing settings, and girls. A tightrope walker climbing a rope stretched between stage and second balcony over the heads of the audience, ending his act spectacularly by sliding down the rope backwards. The small theaters of storytellers and comic dialogue acts. Music halls endlessly featuring girls whose repertoire was confined to singing "Siboney" in Japanese, though before long they were all singing "You Are My Sunshine" and "Deep in the Heart of Texas" in recognizable English. An excellently directed and acted production of *The Cherry Orchard*. A distressing performance of *Madama Butterfly*, in which Pinkerton sang Italian, the others Japanese, and Chocho-san, in wildly excessive joy, strewed the floor with gladiolas. A not bad dramatization of *Crime and Punishment*. A commendable *Midsummer Night's Dream*, an orchestra of ninety playing the Mendelssohn score. Lillian Hellman's *Watch on the Rhine*. A very funny skit by a resident playwright of one of the theaters in Asakusa (the century-old theater center of Tokyo) about women's freedom in a democratic society, so funny that I went backstage to congratulate the writer. Leaving his office, I was guided through the substage, containing the mechanism by which the revolving stage was being moved. Ten old women, pushing, pulling, grunting, were slowly revolving the stage. Ah, Japanese democracy, I thought; liberated women up there on the stage, these poor crones slaving subterraneanly. Matters have changed a good deal since then.

All this energy flowed into the theater from a devastated country in which food was scarce (food-hunting excursions into the country were the housewife's main occupation), in which many seemed to be surviving solely on sweet potatoes and tangerines, in which hordes of homeless slept in railway stations. Where the performers found their energy, why the theater was a necessity, I didn't know. In times of disaster one tries to be cheerful; the Japanese traditionally faced adversity fatalistically, stoically; but this apparently instant recovery of spirit was incredible.

Many of these performances looked very much the same as those one sees in European and American cities and could be judged by the critical attitudes that applied in the West. Most of the plays were, indeed, foreign imports, now thoroughly naturalized, for the process of adopting Western theater had been going on since 1868, when Japan opened itself to Western influence. The productions were, if anything, ideologically in-offensive, neither advocating feudalism (which appeared to be, according to the occupation authorities, what got Japan into the war to begin with) nor democracy (which was to prevent such excesses in the future).

But there were other forms of theater that owed nothing to the West, that were the unalloyed product of Japanese culture, and these, we heard, might well be politically suspect. The Noh, having not changed much since it began, must of necessity be feudalistic. The doll theater and the Kabuki, both dating from the end of the sixteenth century, were stuffed with harmful notions: that loyalty to a master was the basic social obligation, that revenge upon those who had done the master wrong was the most praiseworthy human endeavor, that in its pursuit the sacrifice of family, wife, children, or oneself was a great but not too high price to pay. What was worse, the Japanese military had made an effort to convince the nation that devotion to these attitudes would guarantee winning the war. I wondered if they could have adopted the idea from Hitler's "Whoever wants to understand National Socialist Germany must know Wagner."

The Noh not yet being in operation, we occupied ourselves with the menace of the doll theater and Kabuki. Japanese scholars were consulted, hundreds of plays were read, mulled over, discussed. What we'd heard was indubitably true. Most of the plays, particularly the favorite ones, were based on and bodied forth an unmistakable feudalism and were surely not suitable for people about to renounce war eternally and to become democratized. And so, with the feeling of having satisfactorily completed a hard job, we proscribed the performance of the offensive plays. The same ruthless but requisite extirpation was also being applied to films, magazines, the novel. There was even talk of prohibiting the playing, singing, and, I suppose, whistling of the popular song "China Night," for it had been introduced to the public in a film which demonstrated the benevolence of Japan's invasion of China.

Meanwhile the Noh performers had got themselves organized, were about to begin production, and came around to see what censorship might object to in their repertoire. Having read about the Noh in the books of Arthur Waley and Noël Péri, I had no reason to believe that this esoteric theater would undermine the salutory effects of the occupation. And so I told them to do whatever plays they wished.

Then on a gray, freezing Sunday afternoon in February, along with two Japanese friends who fancied the Noh, I set out in a jeep to see a performance. We drove through miles of bombed and burnt city to an undestroyed suburb where, after making the five or six inquiries necessary to finding any address in Japan, we got to the place—a plain, unpainted, wooden building looking nothing like a theater. It was simply an enclosure for the historic Noh stage, which began its existence out-of-doors, sky above the heads of the audience. Here some two hundred people, mostly middle-aged, were at least protected from the snowfall which seemed imminent, but it was just as cold inside the theater as outside. You felt you were in the open—both the stage and the long passageway leading to it were roofed, three real pine trees were planted along the passageway, a width of gravel lay between the audience and the structure. The stage was austere. The roof and the carving on the beams supporting it suggested an extremely chaste, restrained baroque intricacy; the painted pine tree on the rear wall and the curtain at the end of the passageway were spots of color. Otherwise, plain, bare wood—Japanese cypress—created this elegant, empty place. The stage floor, smooth and polished, could have been a stretch of ice. From offstage came the chilling sound of a high-pitched flute. The musicians and then the men of the chorus numbly took their places, and, the drummers wailing like homeless spirits, the play began.

It moved glacially. The expressionless subordinate actor, it seemed to me, took ten minutes to glide on white-socked feet the length of the passageway to the stage, and the masked principal actor, when he at last appeared, took even longer. A fan was raised, or the actor turned, in his heavy, brocaded costume, as slowly as the rising winter sun. The Noh play, I'd read, picked up speed as it progressed, culminating in a dance by the principal actor. But even when this point was reached, the movement scarcely seemed dance, but rather the first stiff gestures of Galatea as she changed from marble to flesh.

Some years later, reading the works of Zeami (who with his father Kan'ami created the Noh in the late fourteenth century), I remembered this winter afternoon. Writing of the levels of the actor's accomplishment, Zeami uses poetic figures to evoke a sense of these intangible skills. The actor conveys both strength and delicacy: "The metal hammer moves, the precious sword glints coldly." The stillness of the actor is like that of Eliot's still point of the turning world: "Snow piled in a silver bowl." The actor has depth, which in itself implies height: "Snow has covered the thousand mountains; why does one peak remain unwhitened?"[1]

The principal actor stamped his foot, the play was ended. But no one moved, for there was yet his long, slow exit. Like a ghost, which was the role he played, he seemed literally fading from sight. He disappeared, as into the coldness of the grave, and the audience sat silent in the gathering darkness, as though at vespers. Something vaguely religious, ritualistic, had happened, was still happening. Nothing explicit. An evocation, perhaps, not merely of these six-hundred-year-old figures and a historic past, but also of what is timeless.

And then came, in the customary arrangement of a Noh

[1] The translations of Zeami are Donald Keene's.

program, a Kyogen. The master of the household, a feudal lord, must go away for the day, leaving his two male servants in the house. On previous occasions when he's left, they've got drunk. This time, he thinks, he'll prevent their getting at his sakè. He takes a pole about four feet long, holds it at the nape of the neck of one of the servants, and ties the man's hands to it. He ties the other servant's hands behind his back and goes his way, confident that all will be well. But these are a clever pair. Hands-tied-to-the-pole can indeed pick up the wine bowl. Hands-behind-the-back manages to pour from the jug into it, then holds the bowl while the other, on his knees, drinks. And, of course, hands-tied-to-the-pole holds the bowl while hands-behind-the-back drinks. Conviviality grows, dance and drunkenness follow, the master returns, in high dudgeon at being foiled.

The Kyogen was played in a lively, even vaudeville-like way, and the audience no longer looked as though they were at evensong. They brightened up, there was even some subdued laughter.

The effect of the Kyogen following the serious play, I thought, trying to fit all this into Western conceptions of theater, might be comparable with that of the satyr play coming after Greek tragedy. And the performance of the tragedy, like that of the Noh, had a purpose beyond that of simple diversion. It too was a religious observance of a kind difficult for us to sense, impossible for us to re-create. Reading about the Noh theater had not prepared me, except in the most elementary way, for what I had seen. The performance revealed a kind of theater I had not imagined and could not understand, though I felt sure that, as with all great theater, there was more to it than met the eye.

The Kyogen did not end the program. It was to be followed

by another Noh play which, fearing pneumonia, I didn't stay to see. But from time to time for over a year, I went to Noh performances.

What of significance happens in the theater, as all who work in it know, including Zeami, depends not primarily upon architecture and scenic display (two boards and a passion have been thought sufficient for a good actor) nor upon the play performed (a Garrick or a Bernhardt creates engrossing theatrical life out of claptrap; poor actors make *Hamlet* claptrap), nor even upon the philosophical and intellectual concepts of the play (fifth-century Greek concepts are not ours, but we find the plays still viable in the theater). Theater exists when the audience's sense of what life is, or could be, like is validated and intensified by the performance. But the perception of the nature and movement of life is not likely to be first acquired in the theater. To understand what happened in the performing arts, I reasoned, I should look for origins in Japanese behavior, thought, and feeling.

Although I never learned the secret of Japanese vitality (today Tokyo seems to hold more energy than New York), I found what I felt to be legendary precedent for the players of the Woody Herman number and for the vigor and ubiquity of Japanese theater.

The ancient gods had a hard time getting the world going out of chaos, but with the seventh generation the islands of Japan were created, and its creators also produced a sun goddess, Amaterasu, two other children, and Susano-o, a storm god who, pleasing no one, was banished to the land of darkness. Before leaving, he visited heaven to say goodbye to his sister, which he did in a curious and destructive fashion, climaxed by his flaying a piebald colt backwards and throwing it through the roof of Amaterasu's palace. His sister, furious, went into the rock cave of heaven and closed the door. The sun vanished. Here was, for all their difficulties, the greatest crisis the gods had faced. They made her offerings, they sang her hymns of praise, with no success. Then Ame no Uzume, the "heaven-alarming female," thought of something else. She started a fire, and when it was blazing, she overturned a tub, jumped on top of it, bared her breasts, raised her skirts, and, singing an obscene song, danced. Her performance was so cheering that the gods shook heaven with their laughter. Curiosity getting the better of her, Amaterasu opened the door to see what was going on, and an enterprising deity pulled her out of the cave. The godlike way to meet adversity, it seems, is to brighten up the night of despair with lively song and dance. That's the only way to make the sun shine again.

And in this highly industrialized nation, song and dance still have their immemorial uses. The gods are honored, at a Shinto shrine, by sacred dances. At the first planting of rice, evil is warded off, fertility insured, with music and ritual procession. In summer the spirits of the dead are consoled by the young and old of the community dancing in a circle around a drum tower. Nets are pulled from the sea, trees are felled, to rhythmic movement and chant. In the streets of the great cities young men bearing portable shrines dance themselves into a trancelike frenzy. These group celebrations remain necessary observances, as necessary for some as the tea ceremony for others.

The Japanese, it's often been noted, revere their cultural inheritance and seemingly relinquish nothing which at some point in history has pleased them. This predilection convincingly accounts for the preservation of rice-planting ceremonies and of the Noh. But Japan can hardly be described as a nation of antiquarians when, at present, it is the greatest repository of

Western culture in Asia. The traditional forms, rituals, and arts are as necessary to its people as Beethoven and Chopin.

The basic impulse of their art, the Japanese tell us, derives from their love of nature. And they direct our attention to their gardens, to flower arrangements, to dwarf trees, about all of which they have the strongest feelings. Their feelings are equally strong about wrapping up packages handsomely, creating lovely calligraphy, serving up beautifully arranged food on carefully selected china. The conversion of the life of feeling into artistic expression is not restricted in Japan, as it frequently is in the West, to the artist. The professional artist is obviously better at it, but anyone can and does try his hand, if only to learn how to write. He may not produce art, but he's keenly aware of the impulse toward and the desirability of producing it.

That the Japanese love nature cannot be denied. But what is loved is nature rearranged, manipulated, controlled—transformed, that is, into art. And the same process is applied to human nature as it is molded for use in the Noh, the doll theater, and the Kabuki, in which the perception of life is stated in completely stylized forms of gesture, speech, and movement. The forms are in themselves beautiful, but they also serve the purpose of the theater in creating the sense of felt life completely set off from the exigencies and involvements of everyday living.

Watching performances of Kabuki, I became aware that audiences did not come to the theater to celebrate a nostalgic urge to neofeudalism. They came to be delighted by gorgeous costumes and settings, but primarily to see marvelously competent actors explore the shape of feelings, mostly sad ones, of love, of loss, of anguish. (The most frequent cliché in early Japanese poetry: "My sleeve is wet with tears.") The setting forth of these states of being and the audience's tearful response to them could not be undemocratic, for such feelings are the universal lot of sensitive men. The effect of the traditional Japanese theater, it became obvious, was as nonpolitical and, indeed, as nonintellectual as a flower arrangement. Japan had never known a theater of political or propagandistic intent until, after 1868, plays of this kind were imported from the West and imitated, with, it developed, no discernible effect upon Japanese political attitudes.

The Japanese fervor after 1868 for Western art—oil painting music, architecture, as well as theater—cannot be explained merely as the effort to become a modern nation by mimicking the West nor as a renunciation of things Japanese. It was, on the contrary, an exercise, in a strange but pleasantly enlarged sphere, of a historic characteristic: the search for and exploration of new modes of sensibility and their artistic statement in necessarily new forms. A substantial part of Japanese culture had its origin in arts borrowed from other countries, transformed into native expression. The plasticity of nineteenth-century oil painting offered a way of seeing unknown in traditional "flat" painting. Symphonies opened up a totally different realm of musical thought. Victorian architecture brought with it new ideas of defining space. The characters of Ibsen and Shaw moved in an expanded world of activity, and the requisite Western manner of staging the plays introduced alien conceptions of stage space and decoration. The historic modes of feeling were not lost; they were augmented as, for example, when Prussian blue, a pigment imported from the West, was added to the range of colors used by printmakers.

The excess of innovation during the Meiji era produced a temporary neglect of some native art. Kabuki actors took to playing newfangled pieces about contemporary life, and the Noh, dwindling to obscurity, was kept alive chiefly through the

devotion of a lone actor, Umewaka Minoru.[2] But Japan re-
covered, as it had done before, its sense of cultural proportion,
and today the traditional theaters thrive—because they are
aesthetically satisfying (even to many who are not Japanese),
because they are unique, purely Japanese, forms of theatrical
expression.

And of these three, the world of the Noh is least immediately
accessible to most Westerners, and, it should be said, to many
Japanese, whose admiration of its cultural eminence does not
extend to their attending performances. It offers none of the
usually anticipated pleasures of the theater, neither tears, belly
laughs, nor thrills of fear. (The demons, wrote Zeami, should be
beautiful to look at, not frightening.) There are no scenic
delights, no lighting effects. There are no actresses. There is no
sexual solicitation whatever. One should expect and even find
necessary to eventual enjoyment, it's been said, a certain degree
of boredom.

Among Westerners, one of the chief hindrances to understanding is the still fairly widespread notion that plays are a
variety of literature and, as is manifestly the case with Shakespeare, can often be better appreciated by reading than by
seeing them performed. Kyogen and Noh plays, even in the
most skillful translations, seem scrappy. The Kyogen emerge
as rather simple-minded skits, the Noh plays as fragmentary
episodes patched together out of bits of poetry—serious, but not
tragedy (unless the word is reduced to the journalist's use of it),
as the Kyogen are amusing, but not comedy.

Westerners are inclined to think of comedy and tragedy as
archetypal forms, and some have suggested that the Noh theater
offers analogies with that of the Greeks. The Kyogen are

---

[2] All Japanese personal names in this book are given in Japanese order:
surname first, given name last.

sprightly; at times showing the commoner outwitting his master, they exhibit a simple kind of social criticism. The Noh plays are profoundly serious, underlaid with religious, even mythic concepts; there's music, dance, a chorus. But these parallels cannot be further extended. The Kyogen have neither the biting social rage nor the vital obscenity of Aristophanes; the Noh plays have neither the characters nor the structure of tragedy.

The scripts of the Noh theater are no more than scenarios for the performance, so some Japanese scholars say. (They have enormous interest for students of cultural history and of language, but these are matters quite different from literature.) Like the Kabuki, the doll theater, and most traditional Asian theater, the Noh cannot be artificially divided into the "form" of its presentation on the stage and the "content" of its words. It is, in this way, not unlike opera, a presumably valid theater form. The libretti of Verdi and Wagner have, demonstrably, no literary value, though the words serve the purposes of the opera well enough and give a rough indication of what happens in performance. (It is' not unusual to see members of the Noh audience following the performance script in hand, as opera aficionados often do.) The Noh exists only in performance, for the techniques of production, exquisitely refined and polished over the centuries, are the means by and through which its special kind of theatrical expressiveness is created.

It is not difficult to find forms in the Western theater whose effect is much like that of the Kyogen—medieval farce, *commedia dell'arte,* even the antics of circus clowns—in all of which theatrical effectiveness depended, as it does in the Kyogen, more upon the pantomimic skill of the actor than upon the script or scenario. Western drama provides no such plausible parallels with the serious Noh play, for it takes place in an area which the theater of the West only briefly ventures into. Ours is, on the whole, a theater of action, in which the characters are realized in their involvement with other characters, with events, with the here and now. Only infrequently do they pause, as Hamlet does, withdrawing from the immediacy of action in order to reflect upon it, to consider the effect of the flow of the past into the present, to contemplate the shape of the future. This realm of Wordsworthian "emotion recollected in tranquillity" is the genesis of the Noh play and its performance.

By quite different means, the Noh serves a purpose analogous to that of the tea ceremony: withdrawal from the distractions of a busy, crowded, gregarious country into ceremonious quietness, in which there is space and time enough to look, calmly and with dignity, upon a few simple, beautiful objects and actions. If the Noh can be described in a phrase, it is a theater of contemplation.

In Japanese classification one category is "contemporary plays" (*genzai-mono*), but even these give no impression of happening in a world of real men. They come closer than the other plays, perhaps, to having a plot, to telling a story, but the Noh performance puts their events on a plane remote from everyday life. *Aoi no Ue,* for example, tells of the possession of a woman by a jealous spirit; she is not represented by an actor, but by a kimono which lies on the stage floor. When the suggestion of literal objects is required, the objects must undergo a theatrical transformation—a boat is reduced to the outline of its form, a palanquin is diminished to a small bamboo framework, the moon rises in the manipulation of a fan. The actor's face, his chief means of expression in the Western theater, is obliterated by a mask or by resolute expressionlessness. The movement and gesture of the actor, exempt from the strictures of actual time and space, are slowed to the point at which they can be contemplated, not merely seen. Although the structure of the Noh performance is built upon variations in and a gradual increase of the tempo, only in the final dance of a demon play (the last on the traditional program) is there a sense of vital movement. The dramatic personages, thus presented, similarly invite the detached contemplation of the audience. Since they are not, in the Western sense, characters, but types (and are so conceived by the actors), empathic involvement, as with actors who portray "real people," is impossible.

In most Noh plays the *personae* are beyond life. They are immortal gods. They are dead warriors, dead murderers, dead lovers, whose inability to free themselves from their pasts binds them, as ghosts, to the world of appearances. All that is left of them is memory—not the encyclopedic memory of Proust, recapturing the past by re-creating its smallest details—but the essence of the experience of having lived, the cognition of what remains when the activity of life is over. How it was to have killed one's enemy, to have been proud and beautiful, to have lost a child, to have loved. As calmly and slowly as the play moves, the figures of the dead meditate upon the past, and the audience, meditating upon the figures, contemplates this view of life. All is flux, change, evanescence. Attachment to life, even to the memory of passion, is pain. To be done with living, with the "chain of causation" which binds one to life, is felicity.

And these plays are followed by Kyogen.

The primal, still powerful gods of field, sea, and wind depart; the comic servants come on. The spirit of a warrior is chained to the remembrance of the great battle in which he was killed; a husband contrives, for a few hours, to deceive his termagant wife. The ghosts of two sisters cling to the seashore where a nobleman loved them; a servingman goes fishing for a beautiful girl, hooks an ugly one. A grief-crazed woman searches for her lost, dead child; an animal trainer trembles for the safety of his pet monkey. The power of the good subdues demonic evil.

These dramatic images of being pulse in rhythmic alternation. Sorrow is summoned up from the past, reflected upon, becomes timeless entity. Man, the fool, acts out his inherent absurdities. And, at the very end, the courageous prevail against their demons.

The world of the Noh, once entered, no longer seems remote. It's like life.

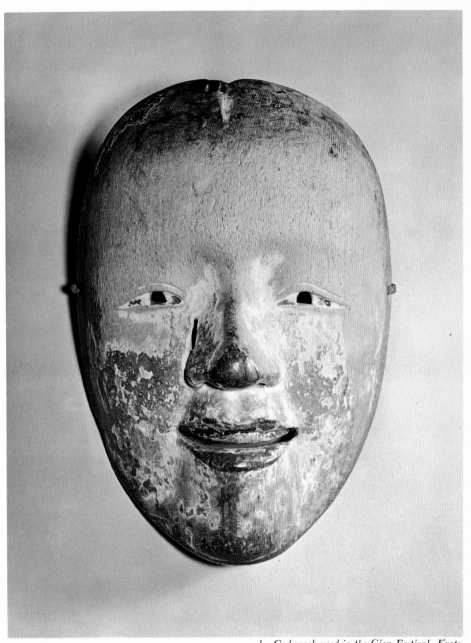

1. God mask used in the Gion Festival, Kyoto

2. *Goto Tokuzo (foreground) as the ghost of Kiyotsune in* Kiyotsune

3. *Kanze Hisao as the god of thunder in* Kamo

4. Kimura Nobuyuki as the mother in Sumida-gawa

5. *Kanze Motomasa as the angel in* Hagoromo

6. *Kita Minoru (left) as the ghost of Taira Tomomori in* Funa Benkei

7. *Umewaka Masatoshi (left center) as the* ▷
princess in Momiji-gari

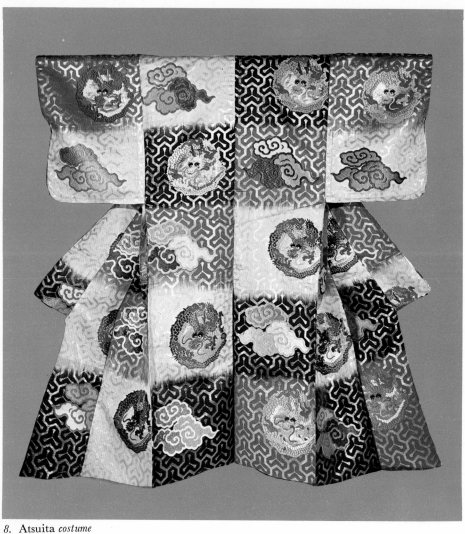

8. Atsuita *costume*

NOH

CHAPTER 1

Noh as a Stage Art

MANY YEARS HAVE PASSED since Noh was discovered by Westerners during the Meiji era (1868–1912). During the early days
following this discovery, interest was limited to only a very few
people, but today Noh has gained recognition from dramatists
the world over.

In 1964, at the East-West Drama Symposium, after a performance of Noh, France's playwright Eugene Ionesco said,
"Japan's Noh is the avant-garde theater of the present. Its
technique is of all ages." A certain Italian stage director said,
"I saw something very basic in Noh, something that we of the
West must have had in the past but have lost. Noh has the basic
characteristics of drama in a strong simple form." These two
men are of the group who earnestly believe that drama must be
expressed in pure form. They were struck with admiration for
the free use of time and space in this symbolic drama form. It
is people like this who make us stop to reconsider the special
characteristics of Noh, its position in world drama history, and
whether or not it expresses anything basic to human life beyond
the boundaries of race and time.

Today Noh is held in great respect among dramatists all over
the world. Not long ago a Noh troupe performed a two-week
season at a memorial festival in honor of Shakespeare, plus
several performances at the World Drama Festival in Paris as
well as appearances in Europe and America.

Paul Claudel, the French playwright, once said, "In Western

29

drama, something happens; in Noh, someone appears." In these few words he deftly expressed the intrinsic nature of Noh. In Western drama, opposition or antagonism between individuals is expressed, whereas Noh is poetic dance-monodrama completely dominated by the leading role, called the *shite*.

Zeami's (1363–1443) plays *Takasago, Kiyotsune,* and *Izutsu* are good examples of cases where someone appears. In *Takasago* (Plate 9), the deity of Sumiyoshi appears as an old man before Tomonari, the guardian of the shrine at Aso. In *Kiyotsune* (Plate 2), the ghost of the warrior Kiyotsune appears before his own wife, and in *Izutsu* (Plate 12), the spirit of the daughter of Ki no Aritsune appears before a traveling priest. Otherworldly characters of this sort often appear in Noh. This type of play is generally referred to as Phantasmal (*mugen*) Noh and was perfected by Zeami.

The structure of Phantasmal Noh includes a climax in which, once more taking the above three plays as examples, the deity of Sumiyoshi performs a felicitous dance extolling the pine and in celebration of peace, Kiyotsune narrates the story of a battle, and Aritsune's daughter dons the hat and cloak of her beloved Narihira and dances in his memory. Constructed of symbolic song and dance, and centered around the reminiscences of the *shite*, the scenes, as they pass from one image to another, demand a great deal of the imagination of the viewer.

The traveling priest who appears at the beginning is very important as a lead into or an introduction to these reflective dramas. The difference in status between the *shite* and the *waki*, as the role of the traveling priest is generically called, is made very clear. In most cases, after the *waki* has given the *shite* his cue, he spends the rest of the time sitting, quietly listening, in a corner of the stage. Even so, the success of a performance depends to a great extent on the acting ability of the *waki*. A capable *waki* can set the play off to a broad and rich development. The *waki,* as an intermediary between the spirit world and reality, represented a most welcome savior for the masses in medieval times who constantly prayed for release from the sufferings of this life and admittance into the Pure Land (*jodo*) after death. While the Noh stressed that suffering awaited wrongdoers in the shadowy kingdom of the afterworld, it also showed that souls could be saved from the tortures of hell by belief in religion and the reciting of sutras. The *waki* was the one who could offer repose and salvation.

When a being not of this world appears, his entrance is accompanied by the music of the orchestra, called *hayashi.* He appears on the stage almost as though he had been called by the tones of the flute and the sharp clap of the drum. The entrance music often reminds one of the chanting of a priest. It is easy to get lost in the illusion that the *shite* actually comes flying into our three-dimensional world from the world of spirits. If there is actually a world of spirits, it is more than likely four-dimensional. This fourth dimension is not for the purpose of setting up positions in time and space as we know them.

Let us consider a creature which can move only in a straight line. All that is necessary to determine the position of this creature is to set up a standard for measurement, after which it is simply a matter of measuring the distance mathematically along the straight line. This world of the straight line is one-dimensional space. The position of a creature which can move in any direction on a flat plane can be determined by drawing two straight lines which intersect at its position. This is two-dimensional space. In the same way, the space in which we human beings move is measured by three lines and is thus three-dimensional space. However, if it were necessary to use four lines to determine the position of a certain creature, that space would be called four-dimensional. The fourth dimension cannot be perceived by the sense of sight as can the first, second, and third dimensions. It is in a very abstract world. If we limit the creature which lives in one-dimensional space at two points, it can no longer move. But the creature living in two-dimensional space can easily move by utilizing movement to either side. Again, if the two-dimensional creature is surrounded by a circle, it has no way to escape, but since we human beings can move up above the level of the plane, we would still be able to move under such circumstances. However, if we are shut up in a room we cannot escape. Let us go one step further and consider a creature which can move in the fourth dimension. Here we have one who can freely move out of or into the enclosed space of a room. We cannot actually see a spirit which has this four-dimensional characteristic, but we can imagine its existence.

Noh presents on the stage a mixture of the third and fourth dimensions which is something different and beyond either. The entrance music plays the part of a medium in the passage of the spirit from the four-dimensional to the three-dimensional world. It has the solemnity necessary for this purpose. At the previously mentioned performance in Paris, a certain Frenchman observed, "This is undoubtedly the kind of scream that brings souls back from the world of the dead." It is said that true art is felt, not understood. In this sense the Frenchman truly experienced Noh and grasped its very essence. The single curtain between the greenroom and the bridgelike passageway to the stage is the boundary between the world of spirits and the real world. Noh makes one feel that even this curtain does not exist.

Aside from Zeami's Phantasmal Noh, there is another group of plays called Present (*genzai*) Noh which deal with actual living people. Antagonism between two human beings is often presented—for example the confrontation between Jinen Koji and a trader in human lives in *Jinen Koji* (Plate 15), and between Benkei and Togashi in *Ataka* (Plate 16). Similar antagonism is seen in such madwoman plays as *Hyakuman* (Plate 119), where, even though the actions of the *shite* enter the realm of the phantasmal, the main point of the play is the search of a temporarily deranged woman for her lost child. The difference between Phantasmal Noh and Present Noh lies in the fact that most Phantasmal Noh plays have a *waki*—a Buddhist priest, a mountain warrior-priest, or a Shinto priest—who lives in the present world, unlike the *shite*, who lives in the world of spirits, while in Present Noh, the *shite* and the *waki* are both characters who are living at the same time. Also in the latter case there is more direct conversation between the *shite* and the *waki*, and thus the *waki* plays a more important part in the action than in Phantasmal Noh. In some cases the *waki* even becomes superior to the *shite* in importance. In the majority of cases, Present Noh plays are much more dramatic in construction. In both styles, however, there is a definite theme which is developed with a strong literary structure.

The plays are also often classified according to their intrinsic character and called Dramatic (*geki*) Noh and Refined (*furyu*) Noh. Classification is based on whether the main point of the piece is the dramatic development or simply a resplendently dazzling presentation. Dramatic Noh includes such pieces as *Jinen Koji, Ataka, Kiyotsune,* and *Izutsu.* The inclusion of the latter two may seem strange when one thinks of the classification "dramatic" in the Western sense of the word, but even those Noh plays in which monologue or reminiscence of a dramatic story by a single character constitutes the major "action" are included in the category of Dramatic Noh. The Refined Noh category includes the elegant *Momiji-gari* (Plate 7) and the virtuoso piece *Hyakuman.*

These classifications, made after Noh had developed through many centuries, were determined by analyzing the themes of existing pieces. It should be remembered that the pieces were not composed with this sort of classification in mind.

Ernest Fenollosa, the man who introduced the arts of Japan to the world during the Meiji era, often spoke of Noh as sculptural in effect. Many others have expressed the same opinion. One reason for this impression is that the Noh stage, unlike the flat "framed" stage of the Kabuki, which produces a pictorial effect, is a square space bounded by four pillars which is viewed from both front and side and thus requires the actor to adjust his performance to this three-dimensional space. His performance must be perfectly balanced, and he must maintain a tension which does not allow any extraneous movement. From the pure white of the *tabi* socks to the perfect curve of the high collar and down once again to the sharp triangular line of the skirt, the Noh costume has a special beauty all its own. If Noh is to be considered sculptural, perhaps it is best compared to a wooden statue. The feet tread the floor of the stage firmly, giving a feeling of weight like that of a huge stone—as though to show positive proof of the great magnetic power in the heart of the earth. Silently the feet progress, seeming to slice across the surface, never losing contact. One is acutely aware of the actual density of the body, but at the same time the quiet movement creates a sense of lightness. The density and weight must project from the heart and mind of the actor.

When viewing a piece of sculpture it is important to remember that it is made up of the fullness of the space it occupies and the space which surrounds it. This surrounding space is rather vague and indefinite, and thus it might be better to say that it has a breadth which links it with the universe. The strongest characteristic of sculpture is that it exists as a definite

9. *Umewaka Manzaburo as the god of Sumiyoshi in Takasago*

10. *Kita Setsuya as the ghost of Minamoto Yoshitsune in* Yashima

11. *Yoshida Nagahiro as the ghost of Taira Tadanori in* Shunzei Tadanori

12. *Kanze Motomasa as the ghost of Ki no Aritsune's daughter in* Izutsu

17   Takagi Koichi as the ghost of the night bird in Nue.

18. *Taneda Michio as the demon in Dojo-ji*

19. *Kita Minoru (left) as the ghost of Fukakusa in Kayoi Komachi*

20. *Honda Hideo as the ghost of a young fisherman in* Fujito

21. *Shimazawa Keijiro as Emma, king of hell, in Ukai*

23. *Kongo Iwao as the dragon god in* Kasuga Ryujin

individual form with limitless space. The space surrounding a piece of sculpture is similar to the blank spaces in a Japanese ink painting, which make a true masterpiece appear larger and more intense than it actually is. Zeami made the following interesting observation on this subject: "There are times when an audience says of an actor, 'He's best when he is doing nothing.' This is due to the secret inner movement of his heart and mind. The two main parts [dance and song] of a play, plus mime, are all performed with the body. The time 'when he is doing nothing' is the spaces between these physical aspects of his acting. The actor's strict care and concentration are the elements which make these still pauses interesting. He must be careful not to lose his intensity even down to the deepest recesses of his heart at such times as the moment after the end of his dance, song, dialogue, gesture, etc. The feeling of concentrated intensity in the depths of the actor's heart is sensed by the audience, and thus the silent pauses are made interesting." When the *shite* is sitting still in the middle of the stage or dancing to the accompaniment of the drums and flute, the perfect intense concentration of his heart and mind create about him an aura which holds the spectator in rapt attention. When this is maintained by the actor, Noh takes on the qualities of a superior piece of sculpture. The *shite* must maintain this aura throughout each moment of his performance. It is not so much his skill in each of the movement patterns (*kata*) but the overall poetic impression he leaves which determines his success. This is what constitutes the aesthetics of Noh.

Several years ago a French cultural delegation including Zadkine the sculptor, Bonnard the painter, and Julien Duvivier the movie director saw a performance of Noh. They astonished the actors and caused a furor in the newspapers by saying, "It was murderously boring!" But the French actor-director Jean-Louis Barrault said, "The quiescence of Noh is like a sigh. It is deeply inspiring." These two very different views adequately express two very important aspects of Noh. For a person who is viewing Noh for the first time, the part of a Noh play called the *iguse*, in which the chorus describes the scene or the emotional conditions of the *shite* while the *shite* himself sits in the middle of the stage, his only movement being an occasional facing toward the *waki*, is undoubtedly extremely boring. However, the degree of interest or boredom of the audience depends entirely on the artistic ability of the *shite*. Even during periods of no outward physical movement, the heart and mind of the actor must be working at full capacity. This is "movement in stillness," an important aspect of Noh.

Modern civilization is highly influenced by speed. The demand for speed in vehicles is logical, but nowadays speed is in demand in music and the graphic arts as well. First the crossing of the Atlantic in one day was accomplished, next it became possible to cross the Pacific in the same short period of time, and now man-made satellites can circle the globe in a matter of minutes, and men have even reached the moon. This is truly the age of the universe. However, when considered as part of the limitless universe, these things are taking place in an extremely small corner of space. The galactic universe with our solar system at its center is a huge discoid approximately fifty thousand light years in diameter and ten thousand light years thick. Outside the galactic system there is an even larger universe in which there are innumerable nebulae. It is impossible to adequately measure this outer world of space with the three-dimensional coordinate system which has been established on this our earth. The previously mentioned mathematical four-dimensional space

can take any point as its center and at the same time is un-
measurable limitless space. One can easily imagine that the
world of spirits is somewhere in the limitless space outside the
galactic universe.

The slow tempo of Noh does not go against the spirit of the
times. The Noh drama partakes of and is part of eternal time
and eternal space. The matters portrayed on the stage are of the
eternal world of nature. Viewed from the macrocosmic point of
view, the infinitesimal creature called man, with his tenacious
attachment to life, spends his days harming others of his kind in
his endless search for momentary happiness. However, when
considered microcosmically, this same phenomenon allows one
to touch upon the very breath of the soul of man. Thus one's
point of view determines whether one is bored or moved by a
performance of Noh. One cannot hear the voice of the soul
unless he sits quietly after the end of a play till the stage has once
more returned to the world of eternal time and space. A performance begins the moment one comes face to face with the
Noh stage, which forces its way out into the audience with no
curtain to hide it from view. From this moment the viewer must
begin his silent vigil and prepare his heart and mind for the
being which will presently appear.

In the realistic theater of the West a drama is acted out completely in front of one's eyes. The position of the viewer is purely
that of a spectator—never more than an onlooker. Noh is often
called a symbolic stage art. The symbolism which the actor
weaves upon the stage is understood, interpreted, and given
meaning by the audience. Noh becomes effective only when
the audience and the actor become perfectly united. In Western
drama the main concern is the actor's ability to actually be-

come the character he is portraying. Noh goes a step further and demands that the performer and the audience become a single entity. Also it is greatly concerned with the human ego. Zeami, in his dissertations on theater, not only considered the audience an absolutely essential element in a drama but also made the following statement: "One's figure seen from the viewpoint of the audience is the 'view from without,' while one's own figure seen with one's own eyes is the 'view from within.' In order to observe oneself with the 'view from without' one must become one with the audience. At that time one will be able to actually see himself clearly." The performer who is able to look at himself from the viewpoint of the audience will be able to get outside himself and see his own performance objectively. Unless the performer can get outside himself and achieve this "view from without," he will never have more than a subjective view of himself. Here we get a glimpse of the sharp perception of this man called Zeami, who chose the colorful life of an artist in an age when the lower classes were threatening to take over and rule the upper. The art theories developed by this great man are themselves great truths of the philosophy of human life. In Europe the theory was that one must delve deep into oneself to discover and present one's true self, but at present it is said that this sort of optimistic self-consciousness will never allow one to understand and express the true nature of man. Today we can appreciate the truth of what Zeami said so many years ago. In order to understand the great praise Noh receives today from people around the world, we must understand the development of Noh and its audiences down through the centuries. The basic character of Noh as a masked song-and-dance drama has not changed, but it has developed beyond its original form and the realm of realism through an organic fusion of song, dance, mime, and the mask. The symbolism in Noh has been refined over a span of six hundred years during which each concrete form was sublimated to a categorical generalization. The difference between Noh in its early stages and as it is today is not in the quality of the symbolism but in its quantity.

Today Noh has gained remarkable popularity among the Japanese. However, just as in the case of the *ukiyo-e* prints, whose value the Japanese had ignored, the first person to recognize the beauty and artistic value of Noh after the Meiji Restoration was a foreigner, the German Perzynski. In 1925 he published a book in German entitled *The Masks of Japan* (Japanische Masken). Interest aroused by this book finally brought about a serious study of Noh masks by Japanese scholars in the early 1930's. After Noh had been "discovered" and highly praised by Westerners, it was rediscovered and, as it were, reimported to Japan as society regained its equilibrium after the Pacific War. With the celebration of the Meiji centenary in 1968, interest in the classics reached a new high. Different aspects of society gain new life and power with the changes of the times, and people look for meaning in life through the things of the past. Noh is not only something perfected in the past but also serves as an important key to history and a new starting point for future development.

CHAPTER 2

Noh History

Origins

"FROM THE VERY BEGINNING, the performing arts have been for the purpose of easing the heart of the poet and pleasing those in all walks of life—the basis for enlarging blessings and promoting long life." Here Zeami indicated that Noh actors (*sarugaku-sha*) of his day thought of Noh itself as a ceremonial blessing. Zeami goes on to say, "Sarugaku [Noh] had its beginnings in the age of the gods. When Amaterasu Omikami [the Shinto sun goddess] shut herself in the cave, all the world became dark. The gods gathered around the door and attempted to soothe the heart of the goddess by performing a *kagura* [Shinto ritual dance]. One of the goddesses decorated a branch of the *sakaki* tree with strips of sacred paper and danced, raising her voice in song. This was the beginning of Sarugaku." Here Zeami has gone back to the well-known myth in the ancient chronicles, the *Kojiki* and the *Nihon Shoki,* in an attempt to place the origin of Noh in the sacred *kagura* dance.

The ancient chronicles tell of the conquering of one tribe after another by the Yamato race until all Japan was united under a single system of laws. The conquered tribes showed their submission to the Yamato court by hanging the bells they used in their festivals on *sakaki* branches, by proclaiming their loyalty and obedience in words of blessing, and by performing

56

kagura-type songs and dances that had been handed down among them since ancient times. The words of blessing were always intoned by the most respected, oldest man (*okina*) in the village. This is the origin of the Okina role and dance.

However, the Okina role in Noh cannot be clearly traced back earlier than the Heian period (794–1185). Zeami says, "The Inatsumi Okina [which used the mask called Okina today], the Yonatsumi Okina [present Sambaso], and the Chichi-no-jo are the three valid forms. These comprise what is today called the *Shiki Samba*. They are patterned after the three *nyorai* Ho, Bo, and O." In this, Zeami is saying that the formal construction of the Noh piece *Okina* at that time included the roles and dances of Chichi-no-jo, Okina, and Samba in that order, and that the roles represented the three Buddhist saints Shakuson, Bunju, and Yakin. As a matter of fact, the Okina dance became one of the rituals of Esoteric Buddhism during the Heian period. It was performed as a prayer by a special priest. Later the Samba role alone came to be performed by a Noh actor. During the Kamakura period (1185–1333) a part called Emmei Kaja was added, together with an introductory dance, and the whole *Okina* piece came to be performed by Noh actors. Finally the introductory dance and the role of the actor who performed it came to be called Senzai, and the roles Emmei Kaja and Chichi-no-jo were eliminated to create the form of *Okina* we know today, which is made up of the roles and dances called Senzai, Okina, and Sambaso in that order.

It is thought that the three characters represented in the present *Okina* existed in Japan even before they were established and defined by Buddhism. The Inatsumi Okina was derived from a dance performed during the Onie Festival, which constituted a supplication for a rich harvest and was held when a new emperor was enthroned. Here we find a case in which a

ritual form from ancient agricultural society has been preserved
on the one hand as a court ceremony and on the other as a
prayer of the farmer for his fields—that is, in the Dengaku,
which is still performed in the provinces. There is also the
Yonatsumi (or Yotsugi) Okina, whose dance represents a
prayer for the generations past and the generations to come.
Chichi-no-jo appears in this dance as the son of the Yonatsumi
Okina, and thus two generations are represented. The words
of blessing pronounced by Chichi-no-jo are for the prosperity
of the home and the generations yet to be born. In this way the
three forms of the Okina dance fulfilled the purpose of the performing arts as defined by Zeami: "for the purpose of easing the
heart of the poet and pleasing those in all walks of life."

In the sixth and seventh centuries the Yamato court was
building a central government and codifying laws, all patterned
after those of China. Buddhism had also been introduced from
China, and along with it came such forms of mainland music
and dance as Gigaku and Bugaku, which employed masked
dancers and were performed at court, and Sangaku, which
served for the amusement of commoners. Bugaku, blended with
the ancient Japanese *kagura* style of dance, greatly enriched the
cultural life of the Yamato court and came to be a part of Gagaku, the official court music adopted in 701. Sangaku included a
broad range of popular attractions, such as acrobatic stunts,
magic tricks, and mime. Pictorial records of early Sangaku
performances can be found on an ancient bow (Plate 31) at the
Shoso-in in Nara and in the *Shinzai Kogaku Zu* (Plates 32, 33),
in which there are drawings of a sword swallower's dance,
sword juggling, a human-pyramid balancing trick, a monkey
jumping through a hoop, and a lion dance. The drawing of a
monkey jumping through a hoop shows an accompanying orchestra which includes a flute, clappers, and a drum. There is

also a gold hoop for the monkey to jump through. The Japanese word for monkey is *saru*, and it is thought that, with the increasing popularity of this type of performance, the name Sangaku gradually changed to Sarugaku, as the performances were later called. At any rate Sangaku was very popular among the common people.

Finally, during the Heian period, when the government of the Fujiwara regents was in full flower, Sangaku began to include more and more elements of the rural dance called Dengaku and completely changed its name to Sarugaku. A document from the middle of the Heian period, written by Fujiwara Akihira (991–1065) and called *Shin Sarugaku Ki* (New Sarugaku Record), describes performances of Sarugaku at the Inari Shrine Festival in Kyoto. It tells of a sort of fortuneteller called *noronji*, dwarf dances, Dengaku, puppet shows, and various forms of juggling and acrobatics. Among these are mime pieces on such themes as "Fukuo the saint searches for his surplice," "Myoko the nun goes out to buy diapers," and "The old man dances in celebration of his new government post while the temple maiden mimics him." In the first there is the humor of a dignified saint frantically searching for his lost surplice; the next satirizes a Buddhist nun, who of course should have no need for diapers, running around trying to buy some; and the last shows the old man dancing with faltering steps in celebration of a government position usually received at a very early age, while the young temple maiden mimics his grimaces and groans. The record also mentions pieces called *The Conditions of Sarugaku* and *The Words of Oko*, both of which titles indicate the use of dialogue.

The above-mentioned pieces suggest new dramatic qualities which were not evident in the older Sangaku. Most of the new plays exploited the various aspects of comedy, and since there are titles for each of the pieces, there must have been some sort of rough script.

This Sarugaku, which was presented at the resting places of the portable shrine during its progress in the festival of the Inari Shrine at Shichijo Horikawa, is said to have been viewed by family groups. Later several theaters seem to have sprung up in these places, and Sarugaku performances were attended by all classes of people. Whether the performers during this period were actual professionals or just ambitious amateurs is hard to determine, but it is certain that they were called by the name of the area where they lived, which indicates that there was at least some sort of troupe organization among them.

Dengaku (Plate 24), which is also mentioned in the *Shin Sarugaku Ki,* had been performed for centuries in the farming society of Japan. When performed at the time of rice planting, it was in the form of prayers for a rich harvest which were officiated over by a priest and involved ceremonial embracing between men and women, or dances symbolizing the chasing off of deer and boars to prevent harm to crops, plus various other dances to appease the gods and bring rain and sunshine. To the aristocrats, who had very little contact with the farming villages, these performances seemed very unusual and fascinating. By the time of the period of government by cloistered emperors toward the end of the Heian period, Dengaku priests from the court formed troupes and began performing Dengaku ceremonies as a sort of group dance (Plate 35). Thus Dengaku became an important part of the festivals of the large shrines in the capital (Plate 34). Finally the aristocrats themselves began to participate in the bawdy dances of Dengaku.

Sarugaku around the end of the Heian period is thought to have been a combination of such Sangaku elements as acrobatic and magic tricks together with humorous mimes and skits.

Elements of popular entertainments of the day (Plates 36–41, 45), including poetry recitation, ballads, *shirabyoshi* dances, recitative *kuse-mai* dances, juggling, narrated picture plays, and priests who sang narrative songs to the accompaniment of a Japanese lute, were all incorporated into Sarugaku performances. During the Kamakura period (1185–1333) two classifications called *rambu* (Plate 44) and *toben* emerged from this conglomeration.

Rambu was the mime-type Sarugaku of the previous age with song and dance elements added. The evidence is not precisely clear, but it seems safe to state that it was made up of song and dance with no set music or choreography, which incorporated elements of every type of song and dance in existence. *Toben* consisted of double-entendre repartee called *shuku*, and stories of the origin of temples and shrines presented as light comic skits. The *shuku* form is indicated in the above-noted piece called *The Words of Oko*.

Furyu was a ceremonial dramatic form which was presented along with *rambu* and *toben* as part of the program called *ennen* for religious festivals and also had a great deal of influence on the subsequent development of Noh. *Lectures on Music and Ceremonies*, which was written in 1440 and belongs to the Hachiman Shrine of the Todai-ji in Nara, gives a detailed account of a *furyu*. It seems to be typical of *furyu* presented during the Kamakura period. The title is *The Excursion of the Great Dynasty-founding Emperor to Lake Suisho*. The dramatis personae include the emperor, the emperor's three retainers, the dragon king, and his three retainers—eight characters in all. The gorgeously decorated properties include a Chinese-style ship, a jeweled mace called Cintamani, crowns for the emperor and the dragon king, and numerous gifts.

First the ship carrying the emperor, his retainers, and the

musicians appears and is rowed to the south side of the stage. The emperor and his retainers debark and identify themselves. After the emperor declares, "I am the great dynasty-founding emperor," his retainers announce their own names: Gicho, Bogenrei, and Guseinan. Next the emperor calls Gicho and says, "Following in the footsteps of my great ancestor Gyoshun, I love my people as my own children and am always thinking only of the peace of my country. I have called you to ask your opinion. This Lake Suisho, as clear and pure as its name [*suisho* means "excellent water" or "crystal"], seems to me to be a fine place to enjoy oneself. What is your opinion?" Gicho responds, "I am most grateful for your gracious words. You, my lord, are indeed a great man. Your benevolence and the wisdom and virtue with which you rule are well known throughout the world. All the people are ever singing your praises. I stand in awe at the important post in your government which has been granted me, and I am always happy for any opportunity to be of service to you. I serve you with fidelity, and I am constantly doing my best to repay the country with humanity and justice. This is an age of happiness and prosperity. I think it most fitting for my lord to view this beautiful Lake Suisho." Then a chorus-like group appears dressed variously as a heron, a carp, a butterfly, a mother-of-pearl shellfish, a frog, a catfish, a horned owl, a crane, a turtle, and a marlin. This entourage is an auspicious omen. Next the dragon king appears and proclaims, "I am the dragon king who lives in the waters of Lake Suisho. This is the precious jewel mace Cintamani. I present it to you." Gicho receives the jeweled mace and presents it to his lord, saying, "The dragon king of this lake presents this jeweled mace to my lord in gratitude for his visit." The emperor responds, "In truth, the appearance of the dragon king is worthy of praise. I accept his gift." Then the emperor and the dragon king are both seated.

Gicho clears the space in front of them and announces, "We will celebrate with music and dance." This Kamakura-period *furyu* is much more dramatic in structure than such *furyu*-like present-day Noh as *Tsuru Kame, Takasago, Seiobo,* and *Tobosaku. Rambu, toben,* and *furyu* were further refined until they developed into Noh and Kyogen as we know them today.

A mutual exchange of material went on between Sarugaku and Dengaku (Plate 47) to the extent that toward the end of the Kamakura period there were still two separate groups of performers, but the material performed was almost exactly the same. In the medieval military saga *Taiheiki* there is a record of subscription Dengaku being performed to raise funds for the Shijo Bridge in Kyoto. In this case the Dengaku troupes, in place of their usual acrobatics and juggling, performed a Sarugaku Noh telling the history of the Hiyoshi Sanno Shrine in which those portraying demons and monkeys were masked and all wore gorgeous costumes like those used in *furyu*. However, acrobatic scenes in which the actors jumped around on the railing of the stage and turned somersaults to the right and left are also described, reminding us that the old Sangaku was still a strong influence. Records of performances of Sarugaku Noh by shrine maidens and Dengaku Noh by Shinto priests at the Kasuga Shrine in Nara during the same period indicate that the exchange of materials had penetrated beyond the realm of professional performers. The Sarugaku Noh performed during this period included an *Okina* composed of an introductory dance called *tsuyu-barai* and dances by the characters Okina, Sambaso, Kaja, and Chichi-no-jo, plus pieces based on stories from the writings of Saigyo, the poet-priest, with such themes as "Sato Norikiyo's visit to the retired emperor Toba when he composed ten *waka* poems to be written on the paper doors and was praised by the emperor himself" and "Izumi Shikibu visited

by Murasaki Shikibu, when she was ill." The Dengaku Noh of the
Shinto priests included such features as juggling, comic dances,
and a piece dramatizing "the tale of a retainer of Emperor
Murakami who was sent to China, where he learned three pieces
from a famous lute player which he brought back and performed
in Japan." The extent of the exchange between Sarugaku and
Dengaku was so great by the end of the Kamakura period that
not long after, during the early years of the Muromachi period
(1338–1573), the Sarugaku actor Kan'ami (1333–84) described
the Dengaku actor Itchu as "a great actor whose style is the
same as my style."

Perfection

ZEAMI REFERRED TO HIS FATHER Kan'ami as "the father of the
art." He described Kan'ami's performance of "the Noh depicting the dance of Shizuka" and "the Noh depicting the
madwoman in the *dainembutsu* Buddhist dance of Saga" as
unsurpassable *yugen* (subtle, profound mystery). The dances
called *kuse mai* from these two plays can still be seen today in
the plays called *Yoshino Shizuka* and *Hyakuman*. Through these
we can still get a glimpse of the "unsurpassable *yugen*" of Kan'a-
mi's great talent as composer and choreographer.

In his *Treatise on Music and the Use of the Voice* (Ongyoku Kowadashi Kuden) Zeami states, "The nucleus of *kuse mai* is rhythm.
Utai [chants and songs], on the other hand, has as its nucleus
the voice, and any rhythm it may have is only for the purpose
of embellishing the voice. *Kuse mai* depends, for its total effect,
on the poses and movements of the body combined with the
singing of the voice. In the past, music for the *kuse mai* and
vocal music were considered absolutely separately, as there was

generally no singing in the *kuse-mai* pieces. In more recent years, however, *kuse mai* became less conservative, even to the extent of adding popular art songs called *kouta-bushi*. The resulting effect was very appealing, and *kuse mai* became extremely popular. This is the main reason my late father began to use *kuse mai* in his Sarugaku Noh, and his use of it was also the main reason for its even more general popularity. *Shirahige* was the first piece in which he used *kuse mai*." Kan'ami combined the best qualities of the previously mentioned *rambu* with the new *kuse mai* and created a new style which clearly set the performing arts off in a new direction.

It seems to have been Zeami's opinion that in his time it was already very hard to differentiate between *kuse mai* and *kouta-bushi*. The *kouta-bushi* had its beginnings in the vulgar popular songs generally called *soka*. This type of song was popular with the early-Muromachi military class, who were the main supporters of Sarugaku Noh, as well as with the common people of Kyoto, who could be heard humming *soka* melodies as they went about their daily tasks. There also developed a sort of patchwork pattern of quotations from classical literature arranged in poetic form and sung to melodies borrowed from the chants of the Tendai sect of Buddhism. All these elements were incorporated around a loose plot, resulting in a sort of music drama which soon crystallized into a form that became known as Yamato Sarugaku.

All shrines and temples after the middle ages hired full-time Dengaku and Sarugaku actors to perform their divine ceremonies and memorial services, and service regulations called *gakuto*, which gave the troupes in service various rights and privileges, were set up. According to these regulations, the head of the troupe not only was given complete rights to carry out all the ceremonies within the temple or shrine itself but, in return for these services, was also given exclusive rights to tour his troupe throughout the area under the jurisdiction of the temple or shrine to which the troupe was attached. It was this system which made it possible for many troupes to perform throughout the provinces. Such troupes included the four famous Yamato Sarugaku troupes: Tobiyama (the present Hosho school of Noh), Yuzaki (present Kanze), Sakato (present Kongo), and Emmai (present Komparu), which were based at the Kofuku-ji in Nara and also served at the Kasuga Shrine in that city. Thus Kan'ami, heading the Yuzaki troupe and performing widely among the common people, was able to develop and polish the basic principles of his art. He was highly praised everywhere he went and eventually began to give occasional performances in Kyoto.

An article written on the occasion of the shogun Ashikaga Yoshimitsu's (1358–1408) first attendance at a performance of Kan'ami's Noh in 1374 reports: "*Okina,* which has always been performed by the oldest actor in the troupe, was the first piece on the program when the shogun attended his first performance at the Imakumano Shrine, and thus it was thought best that the head of the troupe perform in case the shogun might want to ask some questions. . . . Kiyotsugu [Kan'ami] performed the *Okina.* This is the first time this sort of thing has ever been done." As a result of this incident, it became the custom in Yamato Sarugaku troupes for the head of the troupe to perform *Okina.*

At that time Shogun Yoshimitsu was a boy of sixteen, and it seems that he became enamored of Kan'ami's eleven-year-old son Fujiwaka (Zeami's childhood name). Yoshimitsu became more and more infatuated with Fujiwaka and created a scandal among the aristocrats when he made this "love affair" public four years later by sharing his seat with Fujiwaka at the Gion Festival. A certain aristocrat wrote in his diary: "The Yamato

24. Painting: Dengaku rice-planting dance ▷

25. Painting: festival dancers wearing Noh masks

26. *Painting: early Kanze Noh performance*

27. *Painting : Noh stage for the Toyokuni Festival, Kyoto*

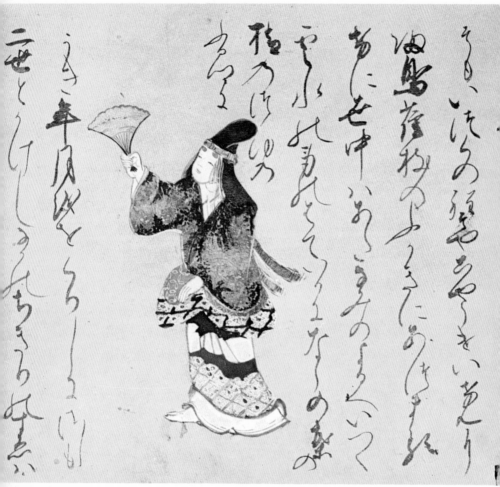

28–29. *Illustrated* utai-bon *for Noh play* Hyakuman

30. *Jo mask carved in 1430*

Sarugaku boy who has been the pet of the shogun for some time shares the shogun's seat and his utensils. Sarugaku performers have always been considered no better than beggars. However, conditions in the world seem to have suddenly changed, for people are now heaping gifts on this boy in order to please the shogun. Even the various daimyo are constantly competing by spending extravagant sums on gifts for him." During this period, even when Sarugaku had become quite popular among the people of Kyoto, it was still thought of as the "work of beggars." The Noh at the Imakumano Shrine was thus a particularly epoch-making event.

Zeami was not only a person of great beauty and a master of Sarugaku at an early age; he was also proficient at games and poetry. He was greatly loved by a high court official named Nijo Yoshimoto, who bestowed on him his official childhood name Fujiwaka and composed a poem for the occasion: "I bestow this name with a prayer for a thousand years of life and happiness for the young bud at the top of the pine."

Under Yoshimitsu's (Plate 53) patronage, Kan'ami and Zeami lived a life of security and ease among the aristocrats and high-ranking warriors. In this atmosphere Zeami reached maturity with the best possible educational background. He was strongly influenced by both Heian aristocratic culture and the Zen sect, which had just begun to gain power at that time. It was these two influences which developed his great passion for simple elegance and *yugen* (subtle, profound mystery). Zeami, in his admonitions to his oldest son, stressed the idea that Sarugaku was originally derived from *kagura* and that therefore its most important elements were song and dance. Elsewhere in his writings he states that Sarugaku is made up of the two main technical elements of song and dance plus three mime elements (aged men, women, warriors). He goes on to explain the mysterious inner element of Noh, which heightens its appeal and effect, with the word *hana,* meaning "flower" or "blossom."

In his work entitled *Fushi Kaden* (The Transmission of the Flower of the Art; Plate 56), which is more commonly known as the *Kadensho,* Zeami wrote, "In this art the love and respect of the public is of utmost necessity to the long life and prosperity of a troupe. . . . In the same way, no matter how skillful an actor may be, without the love and respect of his public he cannot expect a long and successful career. For this reason no matter how small or out of the way the rural town or mountain village where he performed might be, my late father Kan'ami was always most careful to respect and observe the manners and customs as well as the feelings and sensitivities of his audience for each and every performance." Again: "If those of the nobility are scheduled to attend the day's performance, the play should begin as soon as they have been seated. . . . The actor's main object in this case must be to do his best to please the nobles present." In these two statements Zeami expressed the basic attitude a performer must have toward his audience at all times, no matter who they might be. Zeami composed dramas which were appropriate to his environment and education. Thus his plays were of special interest for Yoshimitsu and the aristocrats of his court.

Zeami's accomplishments lie mainly in the field of reflective Phantasmal Noh. His plays were all based on stories from such classics of the prefeudal age as *The Tale of the Heike.* Although mime is so important to Noh that there would be no Noh without it, Zeami's pieces were composed with plots involving beautiful women and warriors in dramatic situations in accordance with his theory that Noh should always be centered around song and dance. His *Kiyotsune, Tadanori,* and *Izutsu* are all excellent examples of Noh centered around the appearance of a spirit. This form is particularly prevalent in the literature of the day. It had elements which appealed to the tastes of both the aristocratic and the warrior classes. It was particularly compatible with the ideas Yoshimitsu was attempting to express in his Kitayama culture—that is, the culture centered around his villa at Kitayama, in Kyoto. Zeami composed a total of fifty pieces, including original works and adaptations of older works.

A contemporary of Zeami's named Miyamasu, who performed mainly in the provinces with his small Sarugaku troupe, composed in a very different style, using *The Tale of the Soga Brothers* and various tales of the medieval hero Yoshitsune as sources for such works as *Chofuku Soga, Youchi Soga, Kosode Soga, Kurama Tengu,* and *Eboshi Ori,* together with folk legends in pieces like *Oeyama.* Miyamasu was typical of the Sarugaku composers in the provinces, whose plays were mainly combinations of characters, situations, and mime embellished with song and dance. It was only Zeami's genius which raised Sarugaku to a level which could meet the high artistic demands of aristocratic tastes. For this reason he was able to develop his talents to the full in the Kitayama culture surrounding him and his patron Yoshimitsu.

Not only Zeami's theories on the composition of Noh but also those concerning production and performance are of superior quality. The previously mentioned *Kadensho* was written around 1400, when he was thirty-seven years old and was enjoying considerable renown under the patronage of Yoshimitsu. It is thought that this document consists mainly of direct quotations from Zeami's father Kan'ami and that therefore Kan'ami's theories on Noh can be found here. It begins by describing the origin of Sarugaku, noting that "the performance of Sarugaku in *ennen* programs [programs for religious festivals] is said by some to have originated in the land of the Buddha [India] and by others to have been handed down since the age of the gods in our own country" and continues with sections on the proper order for learning and practicing Noh at each age level (Nenrai Keiko Jojo); comments on mime and the contents of the various types of plays (Monomane Jojo); questions and answers on performance, the deeper significance of technique, and the attitude of heart and mind necessary to further develop the actor's powers of expression (Mondo Jojo); and essays on the various secrets of the art. In these writings the word *hana*, meaning "flower" or "blossom," often appears. This word is used to express the beauty and mystery which creates interest and touches the heart of the viewer of a performance of Noh. The word was used often by the poet Nijo Yoshimoto, who was a great admirer of Zeami, in speaking of the poetic form called *renga*. The concept of *hana* in poetry and acting was born of and is typical of the artistic taste of the age in which Zeami and Yoshimoto lived.

Between the ages of fifty-five and sixty Zeami wrote *The Seventh Supplement to the Kadensho* (Kaden Dainana Besshi Kuden), *A Treatise on Music and the Use of the Voice* (Ongyoku Kowadashi Kuden), *On Attainment of the Flower* (Shika Dosho), *Diagrams on Song, Dance, and Mime* (Nikyoku Santai Ningyo Zu; Plates 57, 58), and *On the Composition of Noh Scripts* (No Sakusho). However, in one of these works he states, "This supplement contains secrets of the art of Noh which are our family's greatest treasure. These secrets should be passed on to only one heir in each generation. But if one's own son has no talent, the secrets should be revealed to someone else. If there is no one of talent in one's own family, someone outside the family who has talent should be chosen to carry on the traditions of the art. In this way these secrets will be utilized to the fullest extent for the glorious flowering of our art." The tendency to protect one's family knowledge in the arts was especially strong among the aristocrats of Zeami's day, who were rapidly losing economic power. This was the only way they could protect their pride and position. It seems rather strange that Zeami thought this was necessary in the case of Sarugaku because at that time its popularity was definitely on the increase. Later, in his treatise entitled *On Attainment of the Flower,* he states, "There are very few in this day and age whose art is worthy of praise, and our art is threatened more and more every day with total decay. I have set down here an outline of my convictions for fear the basic principles may be neglected, which would doubtless result in the complete decline of Sarugaku. All other secret matters must be taught directly to those who have talent and understanding sufficient to use them effectively." Even so, Zeami's strong belief in his art expressed in his statement "Life will end, but Noh will never die" made of this art something greater and more positive than those other arts and realms of knowledge which the declining aristocracy of his day was desperately trying to save as family secrets.

The Flower Mirror (Kakyo), which Zeami wrote after his sixtieth year, is the culmination of his lifetime of work toward the creation of the art of Noh. In this work he maintains that not only directing and acting ability but also the very structure and beauty of Noh are all born of strict training and practice. It is also in this work that he explains the previously mentioned "view from outside oneself" as well as his famous "One must never lose the heart of a beginner—not even occasionally, not even in old age."

Zeami, whose life had been nothing but smooth sailing, finally met with great unhappiness. Yoshimitsu, who had loved him so greatly, transferred his affection and support to the actor Inuo of the Omi Sarugaku troupe in his later years. Then, in

1408, Yoshimitsu died. Despite these reverses, Zeami was some-
how able to maintain his position for twenty years more. But
Yoshimitsu's successor Yoshimochi (1386–1428) made a favorite
of the Dengaku actor Zoami during his reign, and after his
death, the new shogun Yoshinori (1394–1441) patronized Zeami's nephew Motoshige (later known as On'ami; 1398–1467)
to the extent that he even forbade performances by Zeami and
his son at the retired emperor's palace in 1429. The following
year they also lost to Motoshige the right to perform at the
Daigo Kiyotaki Shrine, and this meant their complete loss
of fortune and position. There seems to be no good explanation
for this complete fall from grace. At any rate it is clear that
Zeami, surrounded by political strife, spent his last years in
misery.

It seems that Motomasa, Zeami's son, later retired to Yamato
(the Nara district), the land of his forefathers. In December of
the same year (1430) he made a pilgrimage to the Amagawa
Benzaiten Shrine in Yoshino and donated the Jo mask (Plate
30) which is kept there to this day, along with the document
declaring his donation. If this mask could speak, it could undoubtedly tell us of the sad plight which prompted this pilgrimage and prayer for help from Benzaiten, the deity of the
performing arts. Two years later, when Motomasa was only
about thirty-nine, he died while on tour at Tsu, in Ise. Zeami
was overcome with grief. Of Motomasa, he wrote, "Though he
was my son, I say he was an unequaled master of the art. . . .
His talent exceeded that of his grandfather Kan'ami. . . . Motomasa's unexpected early death spells the end of our branch of
this art—the immediate collapse of our troupe." Motomasa was
not only talented as a performer; his writing ability was also
formidable. His works, which include *Sumida-gawa, Yoroboshi,*
and *Utaura,* seem to foreshadow his sad fate, for most of them

deal with the tragedy of human life. In these works the strong mime elements of his grandfather Kan'ami are more evident than the *yugen* of his father.

In 1434, Zeami, at the age of seventy-one, was exiled to Sado Island in the Sea of Japan. As he set out on his journey, he left his wife Juchin in the care of his son-in-law Komparu Zenchiku. His lonely life in Sado seems to have been extremely miserable. There are still in existence two letters that he wrote to Zenchiku (Plate 54). In one of them, sent from Sado, he expresses gratitude for a sum of money that Zenchiku had sent him. In this same letter he explains his theory of song, dance, and mime and offers instructions on the performance techniques of the two plays *Saidofu* and *Rikidofu no Oni*. In the other letter he answers questions on the training of a Noh actor. Zeami borrowed a concept taught by Chikuso, the second head priest of the Hogen Temple, which states that the true learning of Buddhist doctrines comes after the doctrines themselves have been memorized—in other words, that real training comes after the attainment of priesthood—and included this in his admonition addressed to the young Zenchiku. He wrote, "Always remember that repetition and practice to polish technique after the technique has been mastered is the most important part of the learning process. Never allow yourself to neglect daily practice to gain an even deeper insight into the principles and techniques of the art."

Sometime previous to this Zeami had been converted to Zen Buddhism and had become a parishioner of the Hogen Temple in Tahara-honcho of Nara Prefecture. During this time he had been instructed in the doctrines of the faith by Chikuso. The teachings of Chikuso greatly influenced not only his personal life but also his artistic theories.

It is interesting to note the change in Zeami's thought and

theories on Noh after he lost his position of influence and power and was exiled. After he fell on hard times, he wrote several more treatises, beginning with *The Flower Mirror* (Kakyo), which was followed in close succession by *A Treatise on Training* (Shudosho), *A Note After the Dream Has Faded* (Yume no Ato Shisshi), and *The Return of the Flower* (Kyakuraige). In place of the word *hana*, which appeared frequently in such early works as his *Kadensho*, he began to use more and more such words as *yugen* and *ran'i* (meaning "fullness," "ripe," or "at the height of one's power"). *Yugen*, which we have defined earlier as "subtle, profound mystery"—a more or less literal definition—has the extended meaning of "highly refined, elegant beauty." *Yugen* was considered one of the basic elements in medieval poetry by such poets as Fujiwara Shunzei, whereas the concept of *ran'i* has more in common with ideas of the poet Teika, Shunzei's son.

Noh itself had seen great changes since the time when the *Kadensho* was written—the time that had brought it to the highest position among the arts of the day. These changes had come about for the most part because of the differences in the tastes of the various shoguns who were the main supporters of Noh, beginning with Yoshimitsu, who was succeeded first by Yoshimochi and then by Yoshinori. Yoshimochi's tastes in Noh were especially refined, and it is safe to say that at least part of the reason for Zeami's changes in theory was a diligent effort to emulate Zoami and regain favor by flattering these tastes.

Thus he developed his theories through one work after another until he completed *A Treatise on Training* (Shudosho), at the end of which he stated, "This is written for the benefit of all the members of the troupe." The statement is in direct opposition to the injunctions in his early works, in which he stressed that the secrets of the art must be passed on to only one heir. It indicates a broadening of view in his old age. It was not

31. *Sections of bow with drawings of Sangaku performers*

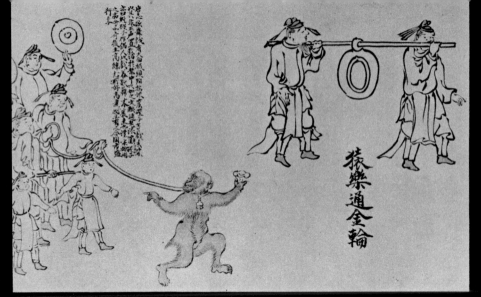

32–33 (top row). *Drawings from* Shinzai Kogaku Zu *showing forms of Sangaku*

34–35. *Drawings showing Dengaku performed at a festival and before a nobleman's residence*

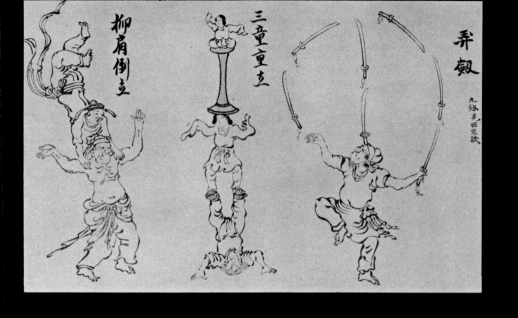

36–37. Paintings: Heian-period dance called gosechi-no-mai

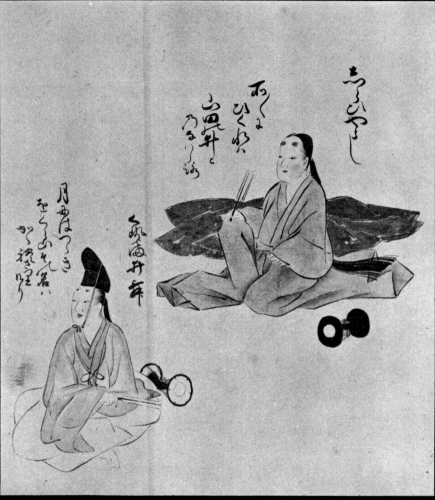

ちうひやうし

わらひくれ
山臾と
なるしゃ

月まほつき
をらうれに名は
から摘つゝ
なり

疾海井年

38. *Painting:* shirabyoshi *dancer and* kuse-mai *dancer*

39. *Painting: performance of medieval* ▷
popular-song genre called imayo

40. *Painting: gourd-beater priest and juggler priest*

41. Painting: man performing sword tricks

42. *Chichi-no-jo mask*

43. *Okina mask*

44. Painting: rambu *(mime-type Sarugaku)*

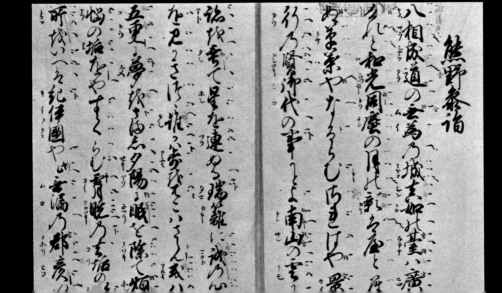

45. Painting: medieval form of dramatic recitation called etoki

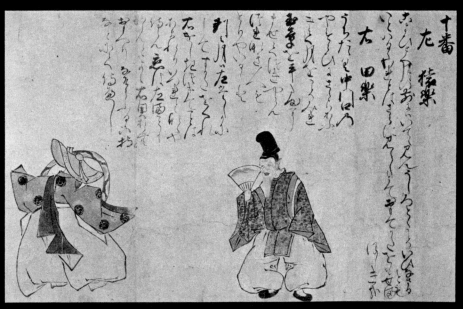

47. Painting: Sarugaku and Dengaku dancers

48. *Sambaso mask*

49. *Demon mask*

50. *Painting:* otabisho *Noh: performance of Noh at one of the resting places of the portable shrine*

51. *Painting:* takigi *(firelight) Noh*

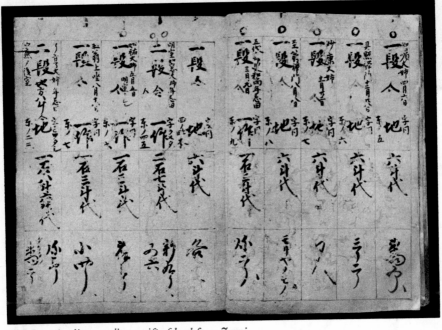

52. *Donation list recording a gift of land from Zeami*

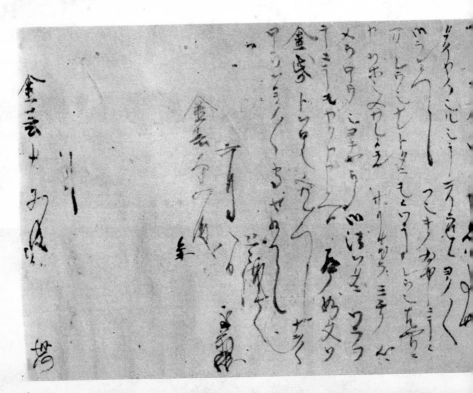

53. *Portrait statue of Ashikaga Yoshimitsu*

54. *Document written in Zeami's hand*

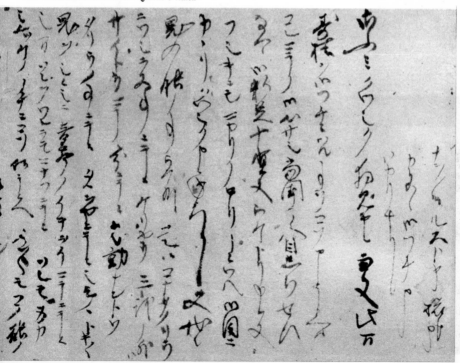

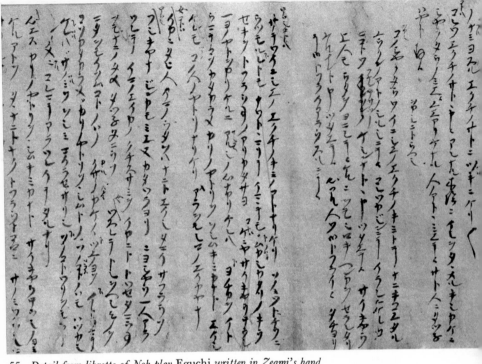

55. *Detail from libretto of Noh play* Eguchi *written in Zeami's hand*

56. *Pages from Zeami's* Fushi Kaden

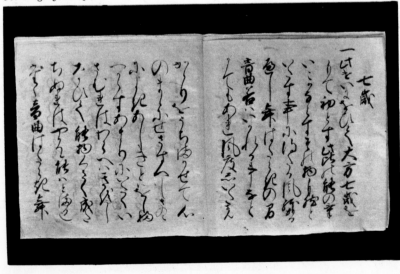

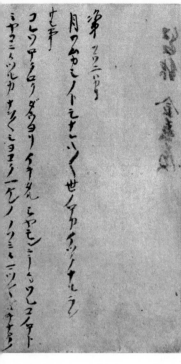

57–58 (right top and bottom). *Details from Zeami's* Diagrams on Song, Dance, and Mime

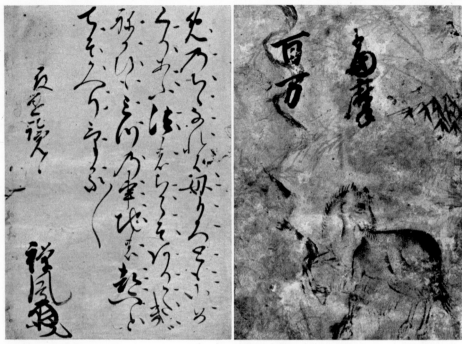

59–60. Last page and front cover of utai-bon *written by Zempo*

61–62. Last page and front cover of utai-bon *written by Kojiro Motoyori*

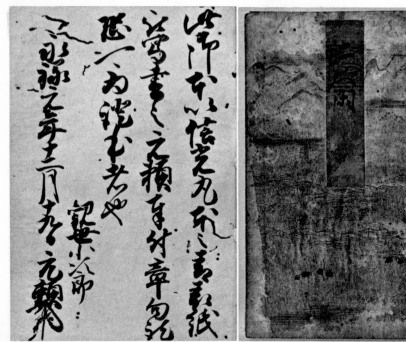

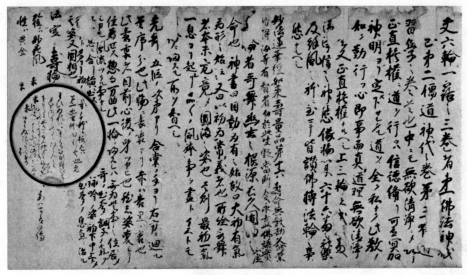

63. *Page from Zenchiku's* Six Blossoms and One Drop of Dew

64. *Stage plan and seating arrangement of patrons for subscription Noh performance in 1464*

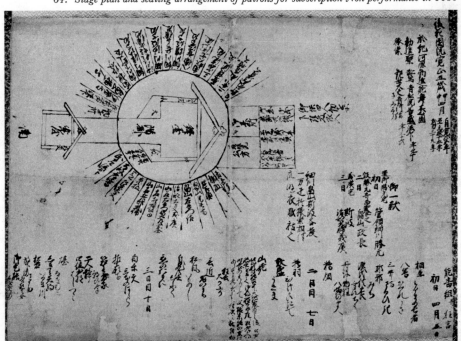

65. Fudo mask

66. *Aku-no-jo mask*

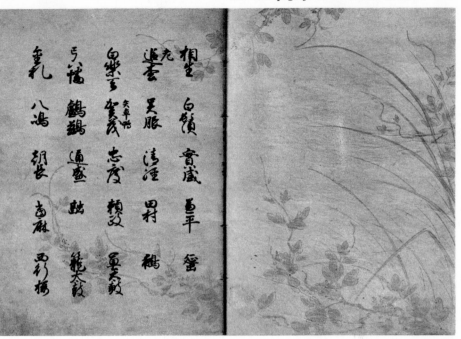

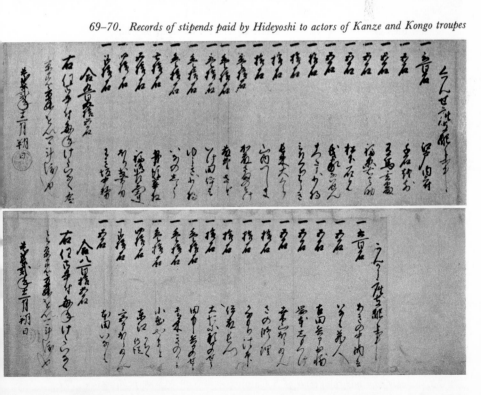

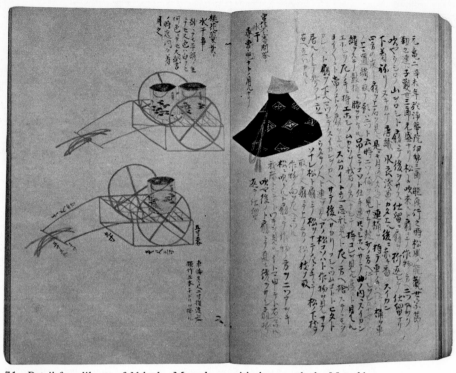

71. Detail from libretto of Noh play Matsukaze *with choreography by Motoaki*

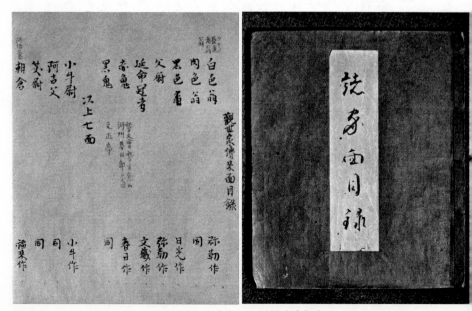

72–73. Sample page and front cover of A Catalogue of Noh Masks, *published in 1771*

74. *Painting:* utai *teacher*

75. *Drawing: eighteenth-century theater for performances of subscription Noh*

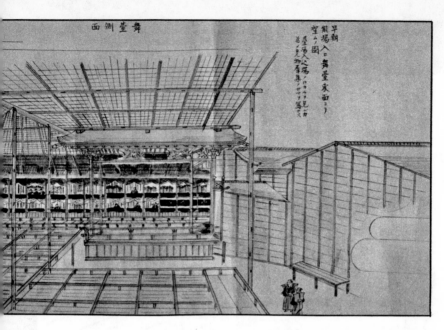

舞壼側面

早朝
能場ヘ舞壼正面ヨリ
望ノ図
壼場ノ人場ハ口ロ十ヨリ見コカ
モ人物客集リサマザ萬ス

76. *Painting: Edo-period performance of Noh for common people*

青貝師

面打

77. *Detail from Edo-period book showing a mask carver*

until the end of the Muromachi period, however, that these secret teachings were actually made available to all Sarugaku actors.

Zenchiku, for whom Zeami expressed great expectations when he said, "He has proper artistic character to carry on the line," did not leave a particularly brilliant record of ability in performance, but he seems to have been a commendable thinker. He was a close friend of the great scholar Ichijo Kaneyoshi, was especially well versed in the principles of Zen Buddhism, and was greatly influenced by poetry, which was considered the highest aesthetic form of the age. In his book entitled *Deep Thoughts on Song and Dance* (Kabu Zuinoki) he expresses the theme of each Noh play with an old *waka* poem and maintains the theory that the ideal situation and the height of art is reached when Noh and poetry become one. He also wrote *Six Blossoms and One Drop of Dew* (Rikurin Ichiro; Plate 63), *The Progression of Five Sounds* (Go-on Shidai), *Five Sounds and Ten Poses* (Go-on Jittei), and *Necessary Aspects of Noh* (Shido Yoso). However, unlike Zeami's works, which were almost all concerned with actual performance and production of Noh based on his own stage experience, Zenchiku's writings were all based on borrowed knowledge from Buddhism and poetics. He often seems to get lost in pure theory. Even so, the pieces he actually composed—for example, *Ugetsu, Basho, Tamakazura,* and *Teika*—have more in common with those composed by Zeami than do those by Motomasa.

On the other hand, Motoshige, who continued to gain favor with Yoshinori and whose position remained secure during the reign of the next shogun, Yoshimasa, left no plays composed by himself, although there are records which praise him highly for his great talent in performance. It is noted of him, for example, that "his rare talent is without equal in the field of Noh" and that "he is without equal in the world." Among these records is one which tells of a gala performance in his later years with his successor Masamori—a presentation of subscription Sarugaku at Kawara for the purpose of collecting funds to repair the Kurama Temple in 1464. The performance was given by order of the shogun Yoshimasa, and one can get an idea of Motoshige's great popularity by looking at the seating arrangement for this performance (Plate 64), which lists the name of the shogun as well as the names of all the prominent nobles and warriors of the day.

Changes

AFTER THE DEATH OF MOTOMASA in 1432 and that of Zeami in 1443, On'ami (Motoshige) and Zenchiku were the main actors in the Kyoto-Nara area. Around the time when they in turn died, the air of the capital began to be filled with unrest which resulted in the Onin Rebellion (1467–77). Masamori and Soin then carried on the tradition. Both seem to have been highly skilled, but they died quite young. As a result of the Onin Rebellion, there are very few records left concerning the lives and activities of these two. In fact, because of the great gap left in performance records of this period, a sizable blank has been left in the history of Noh.

After the rebellion, the Sarugaku troupes found it necessary to make a living by performing subscription Sarugaku for the general public at shrines and temples and by touring the provinces to gain the support of local government officials and the influential people under them. There was a benefit in this, however, for it spread the influence of Noh among the common masses throughout the country.

After Masamori and Soin, the tradition was carried on by Yukishige (1450?–1500?) and Zempo (1454–1532), but because of their youth (both were in their twenties) the responsibility was too great, and a rather difficult period for these young actors ensued. Fortunately Yukishige was carried through the crisis by his father's younger brother Kojiro Nobumitsu (1435–1516). On the other hand, Zempo, who had received a few years' more instruction from his own father and was thus somewhat more experienced than Yukishige, was left completely on his own in Nara when his father died.

Nobumitsu was the seventh son of On'ami and was thirty-five when his older brother Masamori died. He had always performed *waki* roles and played the large drum called the *otsuzumi* to Masamori's *shite*. It was about this time that Noh musicians began to specialize and high-quality instruments began to appear. Articles imported from China were prized, and Nobumitsu's performance on the Chinese drum called the Suhama Drum completely captivated his audiences.

Nobumitsu was not only highly talented in performance but showed considerable ability in composition as well. Numbered among his works are *Ataka, Funa Benkei, Momiji-gari, Kane Maki* (on which the present *Dojo-ji* is based), *Rashomon,* and *Tamanoi,* all of which are still very popular today—even to the extent that a Noh program hardly seems complete without at least one of them included. None of his works fall into the category of Zeami's reflective *yugen* style but are of much more dramatic content in the Present and Furyu styles. His pieces are characterized by the appearance of many characters, the splendor and brilliance of the costumes, the free use of stage properties (all of which contribute to a strengthening of the stage image), the importance of the role of the *waki,* and easily understandable movement throughout. Edo-period Kabuki was strongly influenced by Nobumitsu's works, and it is interesting to note that the works of Zempo, including *Arashiyama, Tobosaku,* and *Ikkaku Sennin,* as well as those composed by Nobumitsu's oldest son, Nobutoshi, such as *Eshima, Oyashiro,* and *Rinzo,* display the characteristics noted above. They are all highly colorful spectacles which appeal to the general public.

The fact that the Sarugaku actors of this period found it necessary to make a living by pleasing the public is probably one of the basic reasons for this tendency in Noh.

With his highly talented uncle Nobumitsu to aid him, Yukishige's troupe, called the Kanze-za, thrived and even finally attracted the two strongest *waki* actors from Zempo's Komparuza. This left Zempo in an even more desperate situation than before, but he stubbornly held his position and continued to perform the sacred Noh for the Kasuga Shrine in Nara, which had been the traditional right of the Komparu troupe since its beginning. The sacred Noh included the *takigi* (firelight) Noh at the Kofuku-ji (also in Nara) and both the *otabisho* Noh (performed at the resting places of the portable shrine) and the *takigi* Noh at the Wakamiya Festival of the Kasuga Shrine (Plates 50, 51). These had always been important yearly events for the four Yamato Sarugaku troupes. Even if they should happen to be on tour in the provinces, it was an unwritten rule that all troupes must return to participate in these sacred festivals. Though there were many troupes which did not follow this rule, the fact that Zempo never shirked his duty even in times of personal crisis is quite commendable. After the death of the shogun Yoshimasa, Zempo returned to the capital, regained his former position, and continued a brilliant career. Besides the plays he composed, he also left some quite concrete advice on performance techniques in his two works called *Personal Principles of No More Significance than the End of a Hair* (Motan Shichinsho) and *Notes on the Back of a Scrap of Paper* (Hogo Ura no Sho), as well as *Talks with Zempo* (Zempo Zodan), which gives a clear picture of the private lives of Sarugaku actors of his day. Possibly it was because of the turbulent days in which he lived that he was unable to find time to leave any new theories on the art for later generations. We may wonder why he did not, for it was during this period that there began to appear treatises on methods of singing and playing the *hayashi* (Noh music) instruments—evidence not only that Noh techniques had become quite refined but also that they were starting on the road toward fixed stylization.

Among those who warmly supported Zempo during his time of troubles were Furuichi Sumitane—famous as a man of refined tastes, as the leading disciple of the famous tea master Murata Juko, and as one of the main supporting pillars among the parishioners of the Kofuku-ji—and other influential men in Nara. According to *Talks with Zempo*, he wrote songs (*koutai*) for these people. In the same book he relates many amusing anecdotes concerning the lessons on Noh chanting and singing which he taught.

Beginning around the end of the Onin Rebellion, amateur performances of Sarugaku became quite popular. The Sarugaku performed by amateurs came to be called Te-sarugaku. Before the rebellion there had been a group of servant-class people employed by the court who performed on an amateur level, but after the rebellion the performing of Te-sarugaku became the fad among the townspeople as well as the aristocrats, the military class, and the monks and priests. The fad even spread to the villages in the provinces. In the towns these amateur performances came to be known as Town (*machi*) Noh or Crossroads (*tsuji*) Noh. Those people of the capital who performed for the court continued to be referred to as Te-sarugaku actors, and at a later period began to form troupes such as the Shibuya, the Toraya, and the Sasaya, thus giving the amateur Te-sarugaku a rather professional tone.

The reason for the popularity of these new troupes and the strengthening of this tendency toward professionalism is probably that the performances of the Te-sarugaku troupes had much more freshness and spontaneity than those of the four traditional professional troupes. Of course one of the basic reasons was that, after the Onin Rebellion, Kyoto suddenly changed to a town of the common people. These comparatively uneducated people were much more interested in performances that were full of life and easy to understand than in the Noh developed by Zeami, which required a certain level of education to appreciate. In order to protect the four professional troupes, the shogunate put a ban on Te-sarugaku performances, but this did not stop the amateurs. At a much later date, groups of child Sarugaku performers and finally even female Sarugaku and Kyogen troupes were formed. Thus general interest in the more sensual forms of drama became stronger. This development was of course one of the reasons for the previously mentioned tendency toward dramatic spectacle among even the actors of the four troupes, as displayed in the works of Nobumitsu, Zempo, and Nagatoshi. In a word, they had to make a living and therefore could not ignore the desires of the public.

It was about this time that *utai-bon* (books of Noh songs and chants) began to appear, and it is thought that this development resulted from the rise in popularity of the Te-sarugaku troupes. The learning of *utai* (Noh songs and chants) came to be considered an indispensable part of the education of aristocrats, and *utai* study groups were organized and regularly attended by those of the military class and the more highly educated townspeople. The fact that the Sarugaku actors compiled *utai-bon* and spent a great deal of time teaching amateur groups tells us much about their lives during this period, and it is interesting to note that the oldest *utai-bon* in existence was written by Zempo himself (Plates 59, 60).

Before Nobumitsu and Zempo died in the early 1500's, Japan had already entered the Sengoku era, the century-long age of civil strife that was to end only in 1600. The shogunate, which had been supporting the Sarugaku troupes, gradually lost its political strength and affluence, and the actors found it even more necessary to sell their art to the people in order to make a living. Fortunately the provincial daimyo who had come into power were more than happy to welcome to their domains the nobles, priests, and performers who no longer found it possible to live in the capital. Such additions to their retinues naturally enhanced their positions both culturally and politically. As a result a great provincial culture developed. Also to be noted is the development of the guilds called *miya-za*, which served the purpose of organizing the sacred ceremonies and festivals in the villages in the various daimyo fiefs. The larger of these villages of course had actual shrines and temples where the professional troupes were used for performances during the spring and fall festivals. With the move of the center of culture away from the capital, the number of shrines and temples in the provinces increased, and this development naturally contributed to the prosperity of the Sarugaku troupes and the even wider spread of their popularity. Evidence of this trend can be seen in the fact that Noh masks (Plate 66) once owned by the Yamato Sarugaku troupes have been found in places quite remote from Nara and Kyoto and that shogunate records of the period include requests to the influential rulers of the northern provinces for support of the Kanze-za. It should also be noted that the number of Noh masks contributed to actor troupes by the daimyo of the period suddenly increased. This tells us something of the feeling of unrest and insecurity that made them think it necessary to placate the gods by making contributions to those who performed the sacred rites.

In this way Noh became widely known and appreciated throughout the country. Performances by both the old professional troupes and the newer nonprofessionals assured its continuing existence, and it was passed down to later generations along with the tea ceremony and flower arrangement as an important representative art of Muromachi-period culture. These arts have become the backbone of the traditional Japanese cultural heritage.

Toward the end of the Muromachi period, Yukishige's grandson Sosetsu (1509–83) became head of the Kanze-za, and Zempo's grandson Kyuren (1510–83) took over the Komparuza. The Hosho-za and the Kongo-za, which had been rather inactive up to this time, gained the actors Shigekatsu (?–1572) and Ujimasa (1507–76) respectively. Thus the four troupes began to show their strength again on a level upon which they could compete with the Te-sarugaku troupes.

Sosetsu was only thirteen when he became head of the Komparu troupe upon the death of his father Doken (whose wife was Zempo's daughter), but he was greatly aided by the famous *waki* actor Nagatoshi. Nagatoshi not only helped strengthen the organization of the troupe but also composed plays, taught Sosetsu all the secrets that had been handed down in the Kanze-za, and later helped him gain fame as an actor. It is said that Sosetsu was very skilled in song, dance, and mime and that his ready wit added greatly to the fascination of his performance. He copied all the secret writings of Zeami which had been handed down in the Kanze-za, making them available to a comparatively large number of people for the first time. It is this work of Sosetsu's to which reference was made in the earlier statement that these writings were not made available to Sarugaku actors in general until the end of the Muromachi period. There is also still in existence an *utai-bon* written in Sosetsu's own hand. Here the musical notation is set down alongside the lyrics, and the book itself seems to have been presented to someone as a gift. It should be noted that at this time the Kanze-za's *utai* was very popular not only among the aristocrats and the warrior class but also among the common people of Kyoto. This was especially true of the *waki utai* (Plates 61, 62) composed by Nagatoshi and his son Motoyori (1518–74).

During the period from 1558 to 1570, the Ashikaga shogunate entered a state of serious decline. Around 1571, Sosetsu, who as leader of the Kanze-za was more or less considered the head of the four troupes, finally found it so difficult to make a living in Kyoto that he took his adopted son Motohisa (1536–77) and joined the retinue of the rising military leader Tokugawa Ieyasu in Hamamatsu, several hundred miles east of Kyoto. Thus the *utai* of the Kanze school became popular among the warriors under Ieyasu, and the *shite utai-bon* expanded its influence. We can see in this one of the basic reasons why the Kanze school later came to flourish under the Edo shogunate, which Ieyasu established soon after 1600. Sosetsu probably never dreamed of such an eventuality when he made his original move to Hamamatsu.

Sosetsu's younger brother Shigekatsu was adopted by Hosho Ikkan, who was in the service of the Hojo clan of Odawara and became famous as the great restorer of the old Hosho school, which he developed into a first-class troupe whose tradition is still strong today. He was strongly influenced by his uncle, even to the extent that he once said, "My *Kadensho* is my uncle

Sotan." Shigekatsu developed into every bit as excellent an actor as his older brother. An anecdote of the times tells of his performance of *Dojo-ji*, in which he entered the bell and stayed inside as it was lifted, surprising the audience by leaping out when the bell had reached the ceiling.

Sosetsu of the Kanze school, Shigekatsu of the Hosho school, and their cousin Kyuren of the Komparu school worked together, creating a single remarkably strong troupe. Records concerning Kyuren are very few, possibly because he was overshadowed by his father Sotan, who made frequent stage appearances and was highly praised as an excellent actor. There is, however, the *Diary of Advice Received from Kyuren* (Kyuren e Tou Nikki), written by his disciple Gekan Shoshin, who had been a priest at the Nishi Hongan-ji and later brought the Komparu school to a high level of prosperity. The *Diary* records quotations from Kyuren which indicate that he was quite a scholar on the rites, secrets of technique, and history of the school. It seems that Kyuren was also highly skilled in martial arts. Undoubtedly this interest of his marked the beginning of the close relationship which eventually developed between the Yagyu school of martial arts and the Komparu school of Noh.

Kongo Ujimasa, with these three schools as rivals, proudly advanced into the world of Noh. Up to this time the Kongo school had produced no particularly outstanding actors, and Ujimasa's own outstanding ability, together with the restoration of the Komparu school, enlivened the pages of Noh history. Ujimasa was particularly fond of surprising his audience with feats of skill in acrobatics and the use of the halberd. These and the anecdote concerning Shigekatsu in *Dojo-ji* show that the spectacular was still prevalent in the Noh of this period. It is this type of tradition on which the rather showy techniques evident in the Kongo school even today are based. The following story is told about Ujimasa. He was so impressed with the face of a wooden statue of the god Fudo which belonged to a temple in Nara that he stole it one night, cut off its face, and used it as a mask when he performed *Chofuku Soga* at the imperial palace. After the performance the mask seemed to stick to his face, so that he had a difficult time getting it off. As a result this mask is referred to as the Nikutsuki Fudo (Plate 65) meaning "the Fudo that sticks to flesh." It seems only natural that during this period of great political and social instability there should develop a large number of legends concerning the strange origin and history of various Noh masks. In addition to the story just cited there is an interesting legend about the mask called Magojiro (Plate 79) in the Kongo school. Ujimasa's son Magojiro Hisatsugu is said to have carved this mask in memory of the beauty of his beloved wife, who had died very young. The mask is sometimes called Omokage, meaning "a memory of a face." Its voluptuous beauty can still be appreciated today.

Hideyoshi and Noh .

IN THE LATE SIXTEENTH CENTURY, around the time that Sosetsu, Shigekatsu, Kyuren, and Ujimasa died, the Ashikaga shogunate also ceased to exist. It was finally destroyed completely by the military dictator Oda Nobunaga, who was later treacherously attacked by the forces of one of his generals, Akechi Mitsuhide, and committed suicide at the Honno Temple, near Kyoto. Akechi in turn was killed by the forces of Toyotomi Hideyoshi, who subdued all resistance and established himself as the *de facto* ruler of Japan. After more than a century of civil strife the country now settled down into the golden age of art and culture known as the Momoyama period (1573–1602).

During this time Kyuren's second son, Zenkyoku (1549–1621), enjoyed the patronage of Hideyoshi and thus became the dominant figure in the Noh world. Among the main actors of the four troupes he was not only the oldest but was also superior in ability. He was given a stipend of five hundred *koku* (one *koku* equaled about five bushels) of rice by Hideyoshi to leave his home base in Nara and join forces with him in Osaka. Zenkyoku had inherited a taste for the martial arts from his father which he passed on to his oldest son, Ujikatsu, who became a follower of the Yagyu school. This fact and the many books of secret instructions of the Yagyu school of martial arts which are owned by the Komparu school to this day tell us much about the origin of the simple, virile, refined Komparu acting.

It is said that Hideyoshi saw Noh performed at the imperial court and in the mansions of influential military men and became interested in it about the time he became ruler of the country. In fact, he not only became interested in Noh but became completely addicted to it. His interest was not of the passive type which could be satisfied by simply viewing Noh. He hired Kurematsu Shinkuro of the Komparu school as his teacher and was such an avid student that he progressed at the unprecedented rate of mastering up to fifteen or sixteen plays in fifty days. He even had a portable stage made to carry along when he went to battle in order not to get out of practice. At the time of his attempted conquest of Korea, he set this stage up in his headquarters at Nagoya in Kyushu and not only practiced and took lessons himself but also called the four troupes down to perform to improve the morale of the soldiers. The following year, during three solid days of Noh at the imperial court, Hideyoshi demonstrated his ability and endurance by accomplishing the phenomenal feat of performing in sixteen of the twenty-eight pieces presented. His passion for Noh was at its peak at this time. In a letter to his wife, he wrote, "I want to get home and perform for you as soon as possible." *The Noh Notebook* (No no Tomecho), a record of performances of this period written by Gekan Shoshin, tells us much about the extent of Hideyoshi's ability as a performer.

Hideyoshi finally found himself limited by the existing Noh plays and ordered the composition of ten pieces based on his own life. These plays, in which he himself performed, are referred to as Taiko Noh. They include *Yoshino Hanami, Koya Sankei,* and *Akechi Uchi,* in all of which Hideyoshi himself is the main character. Later he even commissioned a play called *Osaka Rakkyo,* which tells the story of the taking of Osaka Castle. Hideyoshi's use of biographical material naturally served as propaganda to demonstrate his authority and was thus one of the reasons for his great popularity and ever increasing political power. The introduction of such plays was made possible by the fact that the Noh of this period still displayed the same showiness and had the same popular appeal that had been particularly evident in the Noh of the preceding Muromachi period. This free use of contemporary themes in the performing arts was taken advantage of by the foreign missionaries who began to enter the country in large numbers about this time, and they employed these arts for the purpose of propagating Christianity. Thus there appeared a new style of Noh which was referred to as Kirishitan (Christian) Noh. The Taiko Noh of Hideyoshi and the Kirishitan Noh were actually more like Kabuki than Noh as we know it today.

In a consideration of this new movement in Noh, the *furyu* dance must not be forgotten. This style of dance had been popular in the cities and rural areas ever since the Sengoku period, the century or so of civil war that preceded Hideyoshi's coming to power. Especially in the cities, where the entertainment aspect was strong, many forms evolved which took on the names of the areas in which they developed, such as the Karasumaru Dance, the Jokyo Dance, the Muromachi Shu Furyu, etc. These were all very lively, colorful group dances which were usually centered around some large stage-prop-type object. An example of this type of dance can be seen on the folding screen called *Toyokuni Sairei Zu Byobu* (Plate 27), which depicts the festival at the Toyokuni Shrine honoring the sixth anniversary of Hideyoshi's death. The costumes of the towns-people participating in this dance show the essence of Momo-yama culture with their gorgeous Chinese fabrics such as gold brocades and silk damasks. It is thought that the gorgeous costumes seen in Noh today are a direct reflection of the cos-tumes of the townspeople of this period, since, up to this time, outside of those donated by influential people and wealthy temples and shrines, Noh costumes had reflected the warrior-class tastes in their austere colors and patterns. It is also worthy of note in this regard that some of the dancers in the screen painting (Plate 25) are wearing Noh masks and that in the Gion Festival, which was closely connected with the *furyu* dances, themes from Noh were used on the floats and Noh masks were used on the dolls which were carried in the parades. The god mask (Plate 1), which is used to this day on the doll called Shinko Kogo in the Gion Festival, is a masterpiece created in the middle of the Muromachi period. The people who created the *furyu* dances and participated in these festivals were the same people who took *utai* lessons and were the performers of Te-sarugaku. This development of the increasingly gorgeous aspects of Noh and dance is symbolic of the guiden age of Momoyama culture.

Hideyoshi, in his great infatuation with Noh, not only became the main supporter of his favorite troupe, the Komparu-za, but also paid equal stipends (Plate 69, 70) to all the four troupes, thereby giving them sufficient security to devote themselves to the perfection of their art. Thus the Noh troupes once again came under the protection and management of a political power, and this brought about another stage of transformation in the history of Noh. The firelight (*takigi*) Noh, which had almost completely died out, was revived, and Noh-mask sculptors were given encouragement. The red-seal licenses presented to the mask carvers Suminobo and Zekan, which proclaimed them the most expert in the land, are still in existence. Suminobo, in particular, was greatly praised for the masterpieces he created for the Komparu and Kanze troupes when he was called to work with them at Hideyoshi's Nagoya headquarters in Kyushu. In this way Noh entered a period of prosperity in no way inferior to that which it had enjoyed in the early Muromachi period.

Birth of the Kita School

IN THE POWER STRUGGLE that followed Hideyoshi's death in 1598, Tokugawa Ieyasu emerged as the victor. When he became shogun in 1603 and thereby initiated the Edo period (1603–1868), he sponsored a Noh performance to celebrate the occasion. It was the first time in history that Noh had been performed for such a purpose, and it set the precedent for a yearly Noh festival. In fact, Noh became the official ceremonial art (*shikigaku*) of the Tokugawa shogunate, just as Confucianism became the official philosophy of the shogunate-clan system. The establishment of Noh as a ceremonial function of the Tokugawa shogunate was thus a reflection of the Confucian precept which states: "Those who entertain bring peace to the land; those who rule give it order."

For some time before this, Ieyasu had had close relations with the Kanze and Komparu troupes, and it was for this reason that they were the first to be called to Edo, the shogunate capital. In 1609 all the Noh actors who had been under Hideyoshi's patronage and in his service at Osaka Castle received orders from Ieyasu to gather at Sumpu (in the present Shizuoka Prefecture) in preparation for the move to Edo. Thus all the significant Noh actors came under the direct support of Ieyasu. The main actors of the four troupes at the time were Kanze Kokusetsu (1566–1626), then forty-three; Komparu Zenkyoku (1549–1621), sixty; Hosho Tadakatsu (1558–1630), fifty-one; and Kongo Katsuyoshi (1562–1610), forty-seven.

It was about this time that the Kita school was established by a man from the amateur ranks named Shichidayu (1586–1653; Plate 67). He was the son of an Osaka doctor and was given the name Shichidayu, which means "seven-year-old actor," when he danced brilliantly at the age of seven, was discovered by Hideyoshi, and gained Hideyoshi's affection. Eventually he became Komparu Zenkyoku's son-in-law and later joined the Kongo school. His outstanding ability as an actor led to his performance of subscription Noh in both Kyoto and Osaka. After having been summoned to Edo by Ieyasu, he gained the special patronage of Ieyasu's son Hidetada (the second Tokugawa shogun) and in 1618 obtained official recognition for his newly formed Kita school, which took its place alongside the four traditional troupes. The four troupes had always been referred to with the affix *za*, which means "theater," but since the Kita school had originated from the amateur Te-sarugaku tradition, it became known as the Kita-ryu, *ryu* meaning "style." Apparently this new school headed by Shichidayu also had some connection with the Shibuya school of Te-sarugaku. Shichidayu's Noh was described as being "similar to a painting of a whole plum tree in full blossom which seems to fill the largest room." This tells something of his broad, brilliant style of acting, which was aimed at entertaining his audience. It also indicates one of the basic reasons his Noh was welcomed and widely supported by people who had become dissatisfied with the stereotyped styles of the older troupes. Shogun Hidetada's devotion to Shichidayu was extreme. Shichidayu was always in demand in Edo Castle and the mansions of the various daimyo. At the end of the Noh programs there was usually a request from Hidetada or the honored guest of the gathering for an encore by one of the actors who had performed. Requests for Shichidayu to perform in these encores by far outnumbered those for any actor of the other four troupes. The plays requested for these encores usually were pieces like *Kumasaka, Funa Benkei,* and *Jinen Koji,* which were especially appropriate to Shichidayu's acting style. He was particularly proud of his ability in the use of the halberd and in acrobatic stunts.

The other professional actors criticized Shichidayu for his extremely realistic and gaudy style, in which mime elements were particularly strong. They said, for example, "His *shimai* [dance] is much like the dances of Kyogen." Kyogen was particularly popular with the general public at the time and was being severely criticized by Noh enthusiasts as nothing but low clowning, so that comparison to Kyogen was a favorite way to damn gaudy Noh performances. The conservative people of the day thought of Noh as "especially felicitous when performed in accordance with ancient traditions" and as "something which should be carried out according to the etiquette of the past." Not long after Shichidayu's main enthusiast Hidetada died, he was bitterly attacked for his performance of *Sekidera Komachi* at the imperial palace. This piece was treasured to the extent that it was only taught to the master of a school, and Shichidayu's performance of it caused a great furor because of his position as an "amateur" in the eyes of traditionalists. The shogun Iemitsu heard of this uproar and called the heads of the four troupes in for questioning to determine who had taught and given permission to Shichidayu to perform the piece. It was established that he had simply performed it on his own with no one's permission, and he was punished with confinement to quarters for six months. However, the great number of *utai-bon* still in existence entitled *The Shimai Choreography of Shichidayu* (Shichidayu Shimai Tsuke), which were circulated among the general public, indicate the extent of his popularity. Shichidayu, who was born of common stock, raised as a warrior, and gave a fresh aspect to Noh with his complete freedom from rigid form and tradition, can be said to have been the last of the great medieval actors. This incident, brought about in the Noh world by one performance of *Sekidera Komachi*, is an indication of the strict social and political system being developed at the time by the Tokugawa shogunate. Noh after this time entered a one-way road which led to the rapid fixation of style.

Formalization

WITH THE DECLINE IN THE WRITING of Noh plays and the criticism heaped on Shichidayu's new movement, Noh took its first steps on the road to formalization. First the librettos (*utai-bon*) became standardized, and next the choreography.

It has already been mentioned that there were *utai-bon* from the early period written by Komparu Zempo and Kanze Motoyori. By 1596 the *utai-bon*, which had been handwritten up to this time, were being printed. The first printed *utai-bon* were the *Kurumaya-bon* of the Komparu school and the *Koetsu-bon* of the Kanze school. The *Kurumaya-bon* was edited by Torikai Soseki. In this work he used for reference all the librettos that had been written down since Zempo's time. The book was published about the time when Hideyoshi's infatuation with the Komparu school was at its height, and this of course created a great demand for it. The *Koetsu-bon* was written by the versatile artist Hon'ami Koetsu in his inimitable style and published with a deluxe binding which gave it as much decorative as practical value. In April of 1610, a book of Kanze librettos called *Ganwa Uzuki-bon* (named after the year and month of publication) was published with a postscript by Kanze Bokan, who later became famous under the name Kokusetsu. There are many differences in lyrics and melody between this book and the handwritten copies of Kanze librettos which were circulated during the period from 1573 to 1691—clear proof of the broad revisions made by Bokan in the style of the Kanze school. This is the first *utai-bon* in history for which the date of publication is known and the name of the writer is absolutely certain. It was recognized as the most authoritative work, and its influence was strong all the way up to the Meiji era.

As librettos became standardized, commentaries were published, among them such books as the *Utai Sho,* which contained stage directions and choreography, and Gekan Shoshin's *Dobu Sho* (Plate 68), which gave detailed explanations of the costumes for the *shite* and the *waki,* the stage blocking and choreography, and the correct interpretation of each role for seventy different plays. The fact that these books were published and widely sold during the early days of the Edo period is indicative of the interest of the general public at that time in even the technical details of Noh.

This standardization of librettos and choreography as well as general staging and costumes was followed by the forming of a set pattern in the planning of a program of Noh plays. During the Muromachi period it was a fairly well-established custom to begin a program with a felicitous (*waki*) piece, followed by a ghost or warrior (*shura*) piece, but the rest of the plays for a particular program were chosen as seemed appropriate, with no set pattern whatsoever. Also there were always a rather large number of plays in each performance. In a book called *No Hon Sakusha Chumon* there are five classifications under which all pieces were placed: *waki, shura,* woman, demon, and *hitagao,* meaning "unmasked face." These are very similar to the five classifications used today. The *Keicho Kembun Shu,* a book published in the early part of the Edo period, states that the average Noh performance consisted of seven pieces. As soon as Noh became the official property of the Tokugawa shogunate, the number of plays in a program was set at four. In other words, the first three pieces were the same as at present—*waki, shura,* and wig (or woman)—with the fourth being chosen from those of the present fourth (miscellaneous) and fifth (demon and final) groups. This pattern lasted till the end of the Tokugawa period. The reason for the gradual decrease in the number of pieces in any one program was that performance time for one play gradually increased. Performance time during the Muromachi period was about forty minutes, whereas now the average play lasts at least an hour and a half.

Formalization took place not only in the plays themselves but also in the masks and the stage. The present stage, which consists of a six-yard-square main stage area with a one-yard-wide space running across the back to which is attached a long bridgelike passageway called the *hashigakari,* is thought to have originated during the Momoyama period. The two oldest stages in existence, which are at the Nishi Hongan-ji in Kyoto (Plate 121) and the Itsukushima Shrine on the island called Miyajima, were built during this period. It is hard to imagine much formalization in acting and production during the time when Noh was performed virtually at any time and any place. Thus the advent of the stylized stage can be considered one of the main contributing factors in the overall stylization of Noh itself. Stylization of the masks used on this stage was part of the same phenomenon. In documents from the Muromachi period, there are instructions on the use and classification of devil, Okina, and god masks, but almost no mention is made of masks depicting young women and men. However, from the last years of the Muromachi and through the early years of the Momoyama period, both elaborate classification of masks and numerous instructions on their use appear, and we find such phrases as "the heart of the mask" and "bringing the mask to life."

This stylization of Noh was actually just a return to the principles preached by Zeami. For instance, pieces such as *Sotoba Komachi* (Plate 22) and *Momiji-gari* (Plate 7), which had originally been basically gaudy mimes which appealed to the general public, were all reoriented to fit Zeami's ideology. Zeami, who had left the world quite some time before, was, figuratively speaking, reborn during the Tokugawa period.

The main cause of this strict stylization in the arts was the establishment of the shogunate-clan system of government, in which every aspect of society was frozen into a set pattern. Noh, being under the absolute control and complete support of this government, was not able to escape. On the ninth of June in 1647, the shogun Iemitsu published an admonition which clearly defined the limitations set up by the government for Noh actors. It said, in part, "The passing on of the family traditions must not be neglected, the traditions of each school must be strictly adhered to, and no deviations should be allowed in performance. All matters concerning each troupe are the responsibility of the main actor of the troupe and should be under his strict control." Under this system, Noh underwent a change in quality but found the road toward artistic development closed. It was decided that a man could only become a Noh actor by heredity, and the various roles were distributed only to those belonging to the four troupes. This meant that the Noh actor was a member of the shogun's entourage and was given a definite position in the feudalistic hierarchy in which he was allowed to perfect his art surrounded by an atmosphere of warriorlike decorum. Noh actors were ordered to present in writing all the details of the art, including the plays in the repertoire of all the troupes; the writers, history, and staging directions for each play; and an itemized list of all the masks, costumes, etc. owned by each troupe. This not only allowed those in authority to know the troupes down to the smallest detail but also made it possible for the actors themselves to perpetuate the art faithfully without deviation in the smallest detail, giving them an unquestioned criterion by which they were able to polish their acting and staging techniques to finally make Noh an absolutely perfected stage art.

Popularity of Su Utai

IT MUST BE REMEMBERED that along with this strict political system, there were also changes in society which included great commercial and industrial development, resulting in the growth of cities and towns. The learning and performance of Noh had been popular among the daimyo and upper-class warriors of the previous ages, but now the learning of Noh songs and chants only, referred to as *su utai,* became more and more popular among the common citizens. Torikai Sosetsu, who edited the *Kurumaya-bon,* and Toraya Yoshiari, who was involved in the publication of the *Koetsu-bon,* were not only themselves accomplished in *su utai* but were also famous as teachers. The publication of *utai-bon* increased along with advances in printing techniques, with the result that, around the end of the Muromachi period, *su utai* became overwhelmingly popular among the citizens of the larger cities, where the Te-sarugaku tradition was the strongest. The first publication to bear the name of its publisher was an *utai-bon* called the *Kan'ei Tamaya-bon* which appeared between 1624 and 1643. About the same time the old handwritten *Ganwa Uzuki-bon* was printed under the title *Kan'ei Uzuki-bon.* This was only the beginning of a large number of new books and reprints published in the years that followed. By the Genroku era (1688–1703), the number of different *utai-bon* in print had passed the five hundred mark, and collections of excerpts called *ko-utai-bon* were also being published. About this time teachers called *yokyoku-shi* (Plate 74), who specialized in *su utai,* began appearing in the cities and towns. The publication of *utai-bon* was originally centered in Kyoto but gradually spread to Edo and later to Osaka.

In the majority of these books, the melodic notation was that of the Kanze school. The reasons for this were many. First of all, the Kanze school, begun by Zeami and Kan'ami, was originally based in Kyoto, where it was active under the patronage of the Muromachi shogunate. It was also the first group to be associated with the Tokugawa shogunate and maintained its position of leadership among the four troupes throughout this period. Again, the fact that its melodies were the most appealing assured its popularity with the public.

Against this background, the previously mentioned books of

choreography and stage blocking, as well as the commentaries, were republished, this time as printed books. There also appeared a new book worthy of note: *A Catalogue of the Actors of the Four Troupes* (Shiza Yakusha Mokuroku), which was a study of the actors themselves. These were for the most part highly technical works, but by the Genroku era books of educational value for the general public began to appear. Among these was *Educational Diagrams on Noh* (No no Kummo Zui), a purely educational general introduction to Noh. It was divided into chapters such as "Stage Diagrams," "Famous Masks," "Famous Kyogen Masks," "Drawings of Noh Masks," "Drawings of Noh Costumes," "Drawings of Properties Used in Noh," "A List of Performers in Kyoto," and "The Manufacturers of Articles Used in Noh." About the same time a book entitled *An Encyclopedia of Dance* (Bugaku Taizen), which contained the choreography and rhythms for one hundred Noh plays plus general information on the art, was published under the auspices of the Komparu, Kongo, and Kita schools. These books were not particularly profound, but since the information was presented in a concrete style and since this sort of information had never before been generally available, they were highly prized by the people of the time and were in great demand. Later, two more publications were added to the list which also enjoyed broad circulation. They were *Noh Diagrams* (No no Zushiki) and *A Collection of Flowers and Leaves on Dance* (Bugaku Zuiyo Taizen). As indicated by the titles and lists of chapters, these books were made up of diagrams and drawings of the stage, costumes, masks, and properties as well as the actual lyrics along with their melodies, rhythms, and choreography, so that they provided quite a complete knowledge of all aspects of Noh in an inexpensive, easily accessible form.

Utai came to be included more and more in general education

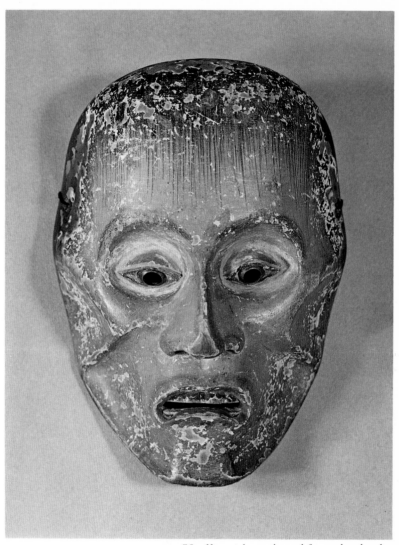

78. Yase-otoko mask, used for aged male roles

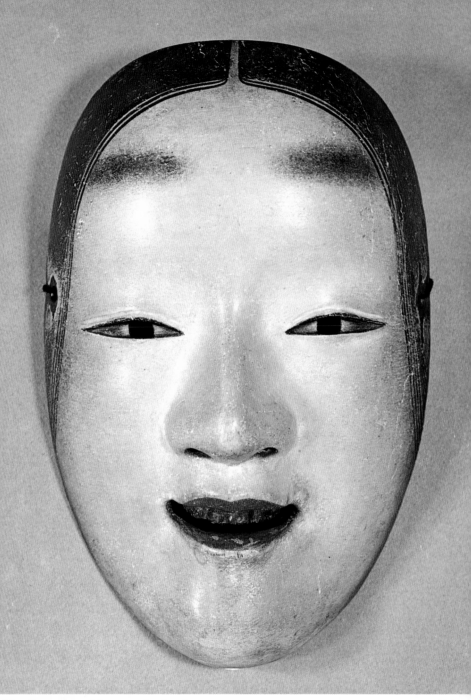

79. Magojiro mask, used for young female roles

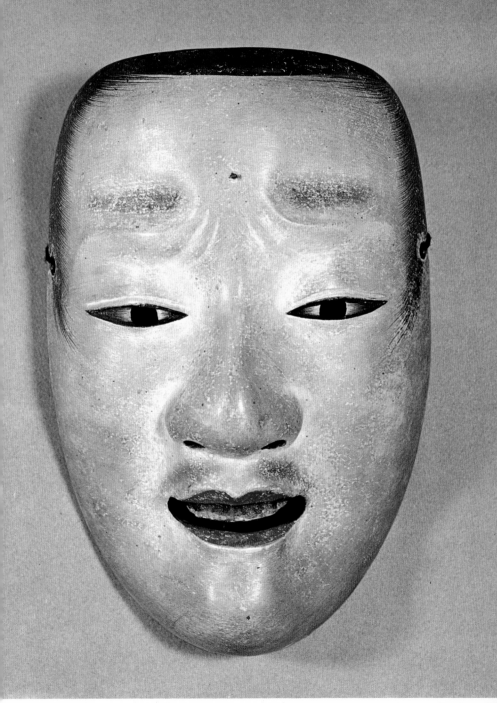

80. *Chujo mask, used for warrior-ghost roles*

81. Cloaklike costume called choken

82. Gold-brocade costume called karaori

83. Musical instruments used in Noh

84. Noh fans ▷

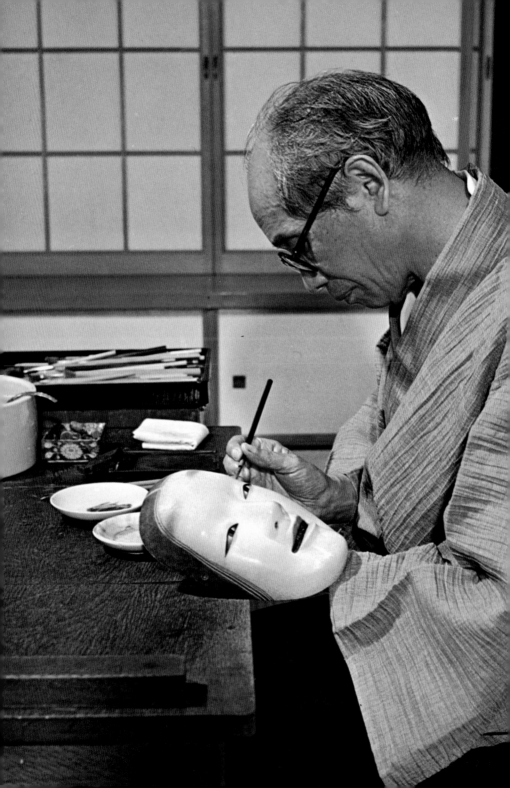

until it began to influence all the arts—to the extent, for example, that themes from Noh began to be used in popular poetry and picture books (Plates 28, 29). It even reached the point where pages were supplied in the *ko-utai-bon* for notes, and a small almanac was inserted. Later *ko-utai* lyrics were used to teach penmanship and reading in the temple schools, which were the public schools of the day. The influence of Noh in all aspects of life during the Edo period was very broad.

From the Eighteenth Century to the Present

IN 1716, WHEN YOSHIMUNE became the eighth Tokugawa shogun, he immediately set about to reform the extravagant policies which had been in effect. His first concern was to take strict measures to deal with the economic crisis which threatened the shogunate. As a result great changes were also seen in the position of Noh and *su utai*, which had enjoyed great prosperity among cultured people during the prosperous days of the last part of the seventeenth century. The Noh actors themselves had to find some way to make a decent living while maintaining the traditions of their art. The change from a peaceful to a strained atmosphere seems to have been a profitable one, artistically speaking, because the following years produced a host of strong, talented actors.

Among them, Motoaki, the sixteenth head of the Kanze school, was a man of singular talent who brought about rational reforms in the stagnated world of Edo-period Noh. He revived subscription Noh, which had not been performed for some one hundred years, and made drastic revisions in the texts of the plays in his *Meiwa Kaisei Utai-bon*, often referred to as simply *Meiwa-bon*. For this book it is said that Yoshimune's second son,

◁ *85. Mask carver Irie Miho at work*

Tayasu Munetake, ordered the lyrics themselves revised by the classical literature scholars Kamo and Kato, after which Motoaki added the melodic notation. The lyrics and melodies were vastly changed, and all the Chinese characters and Japanese syllabary were brought up to date. All phases of production technique were also revised, including choreography, stage blocking, the use of masks and costumes, the measurements of the stage properties, and *ai-kyogen* (interval recitations or performances), as well as the special notes on interpretation called *kogaki*. The fact that Munetake was involved in the preparation of this book and that it was printed by one of the publishers patronized by the government, plus the fact that Motoaki and his younger brother Kiyohisa (1727–82) received an award from the government upon its completion, makes it seem certain that the project was carried out with the endorsement of the shogunate. But the book survived for only nine years after publication. Its short life was probably due to the drastic nature of the revisions it made, and its strong reactionary tendencies. The man who became head of the school after Motoaki's death was afflicted with a terribly poor memory and gave up the post almost immediately. Motoaki's younger brother Kiyohisa took over in his place and became the eighteenth headmaster.

Hidekatsu (?–1812), the fourteenth head of the Hosho school, received official recognition for publication of the Hosho *utaibon* in 1798. Soon afterward the position of instructor to the shogun was taken from the Kanze school and given to the Hosho school. Suddenly, with this new appointment, the Hosho school found itself in a position of influence almost exceeding that of the Kanze school, which had traditionally held the leading place.

Yukan (1799–1863) followed Hidekatsu as head of the Hosho

school. He was allowed to perform a series of subscription Noh for a fifteen-day period outside the palace grounds at Sujichigai-bashi in Edo in 1848.

There were two kinds of subscription Noh: the general and the once-in-a-generation type. The general type could be performed any time there was permission from the shogun, but the once-in-a-generation type, permission for which was granted Yukan, was completely supported by the shogunate and had been allowed only once in the lifetime of headmasters of the Kanze school alone. According to the records, this was actually carried out only four times in history.

The granting of permission and complete support of Yukan's season of performances was an unprecedented exception to the rule. Gaining the shogun's special favor during this period was a matter of life and death for the Noh troupes. For this reason the heads of all the troupes found it necessary to constantly work at full capacity to maintain their positions.

During the Edo period the common people had a chance to view Noh at performances called *machi-iri* Noh (Plate 76), which were held on such special occasions as the accession of a new shogun, the promotion of officials to important positions, the birth of sons into influential families, and the coming-of-age ceremonies for sons of such families. Noh was also publicly performed in connection with important events at the Tosho Shrine in Nikko. The Edo performances were given on the stage inside the grounds of Edo Castle for several days on each occasion, and the general public was allowed to attend on the first day. The number of seats available, performance time, and mode of dress required were announced throughout the city. About 5,000 people were usually granted admission. They were allowed to view the performance from the lawn to the left-hand side of the stage. They were literally packed into the space available with hardly room to stand, and the resulting noise must have been deafening. People who gained admittance were presented with an umbrella when they entered, and were served sakè and other refreshments after the performance, and were given one *mon* in gold a few days later. There must have been great competition among the townspeople to gain permission to view these performances aside from actual interest in Noh. Since the beginning of the Edo period, the common people had been forbidden to take lessons in Noh or to perform it, but with their rise in economic power and their contact with Noh by way of these public performances, some rather excellent performers began to appear among them during the early years of the nineteenth century.

The prosperity that marked the Bunka-Bunsei era (1804–30), producing what Japanese historians have called an "over-mature" culture, came to an end soon after the beginning of the Tempo era (1830–44). The extravagance of the government and society in general had brought about an urgent need for retrenchment, and the situation was aggravated by natural disasters, famine, epidemics, and riots among the peasantry and townsmen. In 1841 the shogun's chief minister, Mizuno Tadakuni, initiated a series of reforms aimed at achieving economic and political stability. Luxury was forbidden, and Mizuno, although he encouraged the martial and the fine arts, at the same time enforced strict economy. His severe orders to the Noh actors began as follows: "To all those belonging to the various troupes: You all seem to have forgotten that your ancestors were beggars who performed in the river beds—people even lower than Dengaku actors. Recently, particularly the *shite* actors among you have become extremely haughty in the claims of high position and ancient noble traditions. You are hereby ordered to remember your origins, recognize your true position in society, and take the appropriate humble attitude." These injunctions were followed by five other orders. The warning must have been quite a shock to those influential people who had been using Noh to gain further power.

The conditions of the times became even more disturbed with the increasing intrusion of foreign vessels in Japanese waters. The climax was reached when the "black ships" of Commodore Perry appeared in Edo Bay in 1853. Now Japan was forced to open her long-closed doors to the West. The shogunate became progressively weaker, and by December 1866, when Tokugawa Yoshinobu acceded as shogun, the whole country was in a turmoil of civil war. Naturally the shogunate no longer had the time nor the means to support Noh.

In 1867 the shogunate was overthrown and restoration of imperial rule was accomplished. For the Noh actors, who in the 500-year-long history of the art had always been supported by influential men and had experienced particularly peaceful security during the Edo period, this change in government must have been a crushing blow. When the deposed shogun Yoshinobu left for Suruga (present Shizuoka Prefecture), the Noh troupes were completely cut off from government support and thus left with no means by which to make a living.

The twenty-third headmaster of the Kanze school, Kiyotaka (1817–88), still faithful to the Tokugawa shogunate, followed Yoshinobu to Suruga but returned to Tokyo in 1874. Hosho Yukan's son Kuro (1837–1917) retired to become first a merchant and then a farmer and finally returned to Tokyo to wait for a change in the times. Komparu Hironari (1829–96) and Kita Katsuyoshi were also in dire circumstances. Kongo Yuiitsu (1815–84) and Umewaka Minoru (of the family of *tsure,* or "companion," actors for the Kanze school) were the only ones who did not give up Noh during these difficult times.

The Kongo school had owned its own theater throughout the Edo period and still maintained it. Before long, Hosho Kuro and Umewaka Minoru began to appear in this theater. At the beginning of the Meiji era it was the only Noh theater in existence, but soon Umewaka Minoru built his own theater and began work toward reviving the world of Noh. Japan was in a period of opening up and developing itself into a modern nation and thus had little time to consider the fate of the traditional arts. Those people who devoted their lives during this period to gaining for Noh the position it holds in society today are indeed worthy of respect.

It was around this time that Iwakura Tomomi, while touring the United States and European countries, began to feel that Japan should utilize its own music and drama, as Western countries used opera, to entertain visiting dignitaries. He decided that Noh was the Japanese stage art most similar to Western opera. This was a happy stroke of luck for the world of Noh. Iwakura began to present programs of Noh for the emperor at his own mansion as soon as he returned to Japan in 1876. This was the beginning of a custom among nobles to present Noh performances for the emperor at their own mansions. Emperor Meiji built a Noh stage in the Aoyama Palace to entertain Empress Dowager Eisho and thereby once again gave Noh the distinction of being a necessary part of all official ceremonies. The long-hoped-for rebirth had finally come about. Now all Noh actors who had been in retirement here and there throughout the country began to return to Tokyo. In 1881 former nobles and clansmen of such prominent families as the Kujo, Bojo, Maeda, Ikeda, and Fujido formed an association for the maintenance and preservation of Noh and made Iwakura Tomomi its head. Their first project was to build a Noh theater in Shiba Park where programs were presented for the emperor, for nobles, for association members, and for various other groups. This association was disbanded in 1896, and the present association called the Noh Gakkai was inaugurated.

Hosho Kuro and Umewaka Minoru, through their artistic as well as their political influence, contributed greatly to the revival of Noh during the first part of the Meiji era. Nor must we forget Sakurama Bamba, a man who succeeded during the same era on the strength of his art alone. Having learned about the new interest in Noh, Bamba moved from distant Kumamoto (in Kyushu) to Tokyo in the same year the first Noh association was formed. His freedom of style made him remarkably successful with the public and helped to bring about a general reawakening to the value of Noh. But the world of Noh suffered a serious loss in 1909 with the death of Umewaka Minoru and again in 1917 with the death of both Hosho Kuro and Sakurama Bamba. These men are still remembered as the three great actors of the Meiji era.

In spite of such losses, Noh continued to flourish and develop. Fine actors with individual styles appeared one after the other: Kanze Motoshige, Sakurama Kintaro, Matsumoto Osamu, Noguchi Masayoshi, Kongo Ujie, Kita Roppeita, Umewaka Manzaburo, Hosho Arata, Umewaka Rokuro, and Komparu Kotaro. The world of Noh survived the difficult period after the Pacific War and is still active and flourishing. What will be the position of Noh, with its deeply classical traditions, in the ultramodern society of the future?

CHAPTER 3

Noh Today

Actor Training

THE ART OF NOH has come down to us through six hundred years of tradition and glory and is still very much alive today. This long survival is of course due chiefly to the strict training and enthusiasm for the art on the part of the actors themselves. The *Kadensho, The Flower Mirror,* and other secret writings by the great master actors of the past emphasize that constant practice is the basic secret for the perfection of Noh. Aspects which must be continually practiced and rehearsed include music, dance, other stage movement, and mime—in other words, all the movement patterns referred to as *kata* by Zeami in his *Diagrams on Song, Dance, and Mime.* While one is learning these, he cannot call the art his own. After the long period of strict training the art must become one with the body and soul of the actor. Even after this has been achieved, he must continue to practice and rehearse all his life. In this way alone can he hope to attain the deeper realms of the art.

Every day in the actor's life begins with practice (Plate 86). As the sun begins to whiten the eastern skies, the actor begins each new day on the stage accompanied only by the spirits of his ancestors and face to face with his own soul. In every sound, in every movement, the actor must, even in rehearsal, give his whole heart in order to reach the goal expressed in the princi-

154

ple: "One who never appears small or weak is a strong *shite;* one who is brilliant in every phase of the art is a *shite* who has attained *yugen.*"

The dictionary tells us that the word *keiko*—literally, "practice," "training," or "rehearsal"—means "learning things handed down from the past." At the beginning of his "Notes on Training at Each Age Level" (Nenrai Keiko Jojo) in the *Kadensho* (Plate 56), Zeami says, "Training in this art should begin about the age of seven." Children sometimes appear in the *kokata* (child) parts at an earlier age, but a Noh actor begins the actual training of his own sons at about the age of seven (Plate 89). This practice may have been the beginning of the general belief in all Japanese traditional arts that the training of a true artist must begin on the sixth day of the sixth month at the age of six. Zeami gave specific instructions for the most effective type of training for every period in an actor's life. For instance, in his instructions to actors in the thirty-four-to-thirty-five age bracket he says, "An actor is at the height of his powers at this age. If he has diligently trained in his early years and mastered to perfection all the techniques he has been taught, he will gain the praise and honor of the whole world."

As in *The Flower Mirror,* Zeami indicates here also that an actor who maintains enthusiasm and freshness in his approach to proper training and performance techniques at every stage in his life as an artist will continue to discover new facets of his art and new methods of expression till the day he dies. Zeami considered this one of the most important secrets to be passed down from generation to generation. For this reason training of students other than professional actors is also strict (Plate 88). For quite some time the National University of Fine Arts has given classes in Noh technique.

These classes are taught by actors of the Kanze and Hosho

schools together with the instrumental performers called *haya-shi-kata,* and the students are given the strictest of training (Plate 87). This is one way in which the government does its part in supporting and carrying on the tradition of this national art. In various ways the truth of Zeami's words, "Life will end, but Noh will never die," has been proved again and again through the centuries. Zeami, who suffered much and finally found clarity of vision through his conversion to Buddhism, left to us many words of wisdom which are applicable not only to Noh but also to human spiritual growth and general education.

Performances in the Noh theaters at the present time consist of regular monthly performances called *tsuki-nami reikai* and special programs called *bekkai* sponsored by the headmaster of each school, as well as regular programs sponsored by various groups. Newspaper companies and Noh study groups also sponsor performances from time to time in other theaters, halls, and outdoor amphitheaters. These performances are almost all held in Tokyo, Kyoto, Osaka, and Nagoya. Very few are given in the provinces—a regrettable situation since it limits the audience and inhibits the further development of Noh as a national art. However, the recent rise in the popularity of Noh among young people and students is extremely encouraging to the actors and those concerned with its future.

This tendency has encouraged a reappraisal of the art by the actors to the extent that they carry on a study in depth from various angles of every piece they perform. First they review all available knowledge on the piece in their own school. The headmaster restudies all the writings and traditions which have been passed down to him (Plate 91). Sakon, former headmaster of the Kanze school, said in his memoirs, "Nothing is more enjoyable to me than studying the various writings of my ancestors, quietly sitting at my desk deep into the night. These books are filled with great truths and profound artistic value. They teach me not only the outward forms of Noh; more importantly, they reveal its very spirit. They give me deeper understanding of the substance and artistic appeal of the plays." Similarly, the present Kanze headmaster, Motomasa, and the headmasters of the other schools are finding that these secret writings are not merely dry lists of the forms of Noh but also reveal the very heart of the development of the art during the last six hundred years. Thus, with a deeper understanding of the art itself, the Noh actors are finally beginning to develop and relate to modern society rather than simply copy traditional forms. The result is more deeply artistic performances by more educated and thus more individualistically talented actors.

Several days before each performance a rehearsal called the *moshi-awase* (Plate 90) is held. It is attended by all those who will participate in the performance, including the *shite*, the *tsure* (companion to the *shite*), the *waki*, the *kyogen-kata* (Kyogen actors), and the *hayashi-kata*. Since the *moshi-awase* is similar to a dress rehearsal, it would seem only natural that a complete run-through of the plays to be performed would be necessary, but at this time only the more important scenes are rehearsed. The reason for not doing a complete run-through is that the lyrics and movements for each play are absolutely set, and if each performer participating has learned his part well, the performance will go smoothly even if all the details are not reviewed together in rehearsal. This custom is a holdover from the days when Noh was the official property of the government and a perfect performance was often demanded at a moment's notice. However, Noh actors of today are beginning to realize that they should place more importance on rehearsals, as is done in modern theater productions, for artistic improvement.

The problem of who should take the responsibility of "directing" these rehearsals is usually solved by giving the *shite* the final word. In medieval Sarugaku troupes the head of the troupe, called the *osa,* and his assistant, called the *gon-no-kami,* were generally busy with managerial duties, so that the responsibilities of a director fell on the shoulders of the leading actor of the troupe, the *tayu.* There are some who maintain that a director as such is not necessary in pure Noh performances. This is a point which requires serious thought when considering the present position of Noh and its development in the future.

Masks

EVEN THOUGH THE MASK used for the *shite* of each play is set by tradition, there is enough variation in different copies of masks of the same name that the whole mood of the performance is determined by the copy of the mask chosen. For instance, the mask used for the madwoman play called *Hyakuman* is either Fukai or Shakumi, depending on the school. These two masks depict the grief-stricken face of a mother who has become slightly deranged in the search for her lost child. The mask used for a given play was not set until the strict formalization of Noh took place during the Edo period. Since that time the Kanze and Hosho schools have used the Fukai mask, while the Komparu, Kongo, and Kita schools use the Shakumi.

The actor gives up his individuality when he puts on the mask, and his interpretation of the part he plays is almost completely governed by the mask he has chosen. In other words, each mask has its own individual *kurai-dori*—that is, "position" or "level of quality"—which must be adhered to and brought to life by the actor's interpretation. This is illustrated by the belief of the actors that "not the person wearing the mask, but the mask itself sees." Different copies of Fukai masks vary the age of the character, while some express deep grief and others express a deep, tender motherly love. Thus it is obvious that the particular mask chosen by the actor for a performance of *Hyakuman* greatly colors the interpretation of the part. When the use of masks of different names is allowed, the possible variations are of course even greater. The Irish poet Yeats expressed the great importance of the mask and the "life" in it which demands a certain interpretation when he said, "Eventually plays will probably be written for the existing masks rather than masks made for use in already written plays."

It is no exaggeration when the actors say, "A Noh play begins with the mask." It seems that the masks first used in Sarugaku were only those which depicted superhuman or extremely unusual beings such as demons, gods, very old men, and people from faraway countries—roles which were necessary for performance of the religious rites and ceremonies from which Saragaku originated. This is the reason for the worshipful attitude expressed toward the masks by the actors even today. For this reason it is thought that the "woman masks" of which Zeami speaks were those used for roles depicting temple maidens and angels only. The necessity for young-man and young-woman masks came about because of Zeami's standardization of the principles of Noh composition, in which he required the *shite* of his Phantasmal Noh to be masked. The early young-man and young-woman masks had bright, cheerful, hopeful expressions full of energy and life. As Noh became more and more involved with the intelligentsia, it began to reflect their elegant tastes and take on an atmosphere of Zen Buddhism. The masks also began to take on a more refined beauty. Later, when Noh became the official property of the strictly feudalistic Tokugawa government, under which it was almost impossible for it to express human emotions and individuality, Noh masks once again began to reflect the new social and cultural system, becoming more and more stylized.

There are about fifty different kinds of masks in use today. Roughly classified, they are masks used in *Okina:* Hakushikijo (Okina) and Kokushikijo (Sambaso); god and demon masks, including Obeshimi, Kobeshimi, Otobide, Kotobide, Shikami, Akujo, Tenjin, Shintai, and Fudo; old-man masks (*jo-men*), including Kouji-jo (or Kojo), Asakura-jo, Sanko-jo, Warai-jo, Akobu-jo, Shiwa-jo, Mai-jo, and Ishio-jo; spirit masks, including Mikazuki, Ayakashi, Yase-otoko, Deigan, Ryo-onna, Yase-onna, Hashihime, Hannya, and Ja; man masks, including Heida, Chu-jo, Kantan-otoko, Imawaka, Juroku, Kasshiki, Yoroboshi, Semimaru, Doji, and Jido; woman masks, including Ko-omote, Waka-onna, Magojiro, Zo-onna, Omi-onna, Fukai, Shakumi, Uba, and Rojo; and special masks used for only one play such as Yorimasa, Shunkan, Kagekiyo, Shojo, and Shishi-guchi (Plates 43, 48, 78–80, 92–107). There are also many parts played without masks. The bare face in this case is called *shitamen.* Make-up is never used in Noh.

Unlike the Buddhist sculptors of earlier days, who were greatly respected and almost partook of the divinity of the images they carved, those who carved Noh masks were people in some way connected with the various troupes. Their social position was not much better than that of the Sarugaku actors themselves. It is thought that by the end of the Muromachi period the general classifications of masks were set to a certain degree. The best of each classification, called the *hommen,* were kept by the headmaster and were faithfully copied when another mask of the same type became necessary. During the Edo period, mask carvers patronized by the government continued the copying, and this of course contributed to further stylization.

Writings left from the end of the Muromachi to the early years of the Edo period show a gradual refinement in attitude toward the masks in such admonitions as "The mask has a soul," "The whole heart and soul of the actor must be concentrated on the mask," "Realization and utilization of the charm and suggestiveness of the mask is of utmost importance." The proper use of the mask was stylized in such set movements as "raise the mask," "lower the mask," "look down from above," "look up," "look down," "look to the right," "look to the left," "look at the flower with the soul," "turn only the mask to look over the left shoulder," "cry with the left hand," and "cry with both hands." With the formalization of choreography these simple directions became fixed, and the words changed to more poetic terms such as *kumorasu* (to shade the face—that is, to look down); *terasu* (to make shine—that is, to look up); *tsukau* (to use) and *kiru* (to cut), indicating movements of the head to left and right; and *shioru* (to wilt or to fade—that is, to cry). In the past these forms were purely stylized movements, but Noh actors use them today along with the *kurai* (level of distinction or quality) of the mask to give it life and expression.

Costumes

WHEN THE MASK TO BE USED has been determined, the next thing that must be decided upon is the proper costume to fit the mask and the play to be performed. Noh costumes are referred to by the word *shozoku* rather than *isho,* the more common word meaning "costume." This is a tradition borrowed from the older Bugaku. The Hosho school's costume orders for the *shite* in *Hyakuman* are: wig, wigband, *mae-ori eboshi* (forward-folded ceremonial lacquered hat), the Shakumi or Fukai mask, *surihaku* (patterned undergarment), *nuihaku* (outer robe), sash, *choken* (loose jacket), fan, and *sasa* (a twig of bamboo always carried by deranged persons in classical Japanese theater). However, the pattern and color of these garments are not designated. A certain amount of leeway is allowed to fit the mask chosen and the interpretation of the actor.

The *shite* first puts on a special kind of underwear which fits close to and covers the whole body. To this he adds pure-white *tabi* socks. Next a padded white undergarment is put on as a base to give the actor's figure an appearance of solidity. Over this goes the *surihaku,* which is made of white silk usually covered with a gold or silver pattern. On top of this comes the *nuihaku* (Plate 115), which is of heavy silk, exquisitely embroidered with birds and flowers. This garment is secured around the waist, but the arms are not inserted in the sleeves, and the top is allowed to hang down in the style called *koshimaki.*

The terms *iro-iri* (with color) and *iro-nashi* (without color) are used in Noh to designate the proper costume according to the age of the female character to be portrayed. *Iro-iri* indicates that the costume includes the color red in its pattern and is limited to use in such pieces as *Yuya* (Plate 13) and *Matsukaze* (Plate 130) in conjunction with the Ko-omote, Magojiro, and Waka-onna masks, which depict beautiful young women. *Iro-nashi* indicates gorgeous patterns using all colors but red and is used to describe costumes worn with the Shakumi and Fukai masks in pieces depicting women between the ages of thirty and forty—for example, the *shite* in *Hyakuman, Sumida-gawa* (Plate 4), and *Kinuta.* The *nuihaku* used for Hyakuman in Plate 115 has broad horizontal stripes of light brown and gray with an even lighter overall woven diamond pattern on top of which are embroidered leaves and blossoms of the water plantain, creating an atmosphere of late spring or early summer. On top of this is worn a

86. *Kanze Motomasa in rehearsal*

87 (left). Kanze Motomasa teaching at the Tokyo University of Fine Arts.   88 (center).
Kanze Motomasa teaching his students at the theater.   89 (right). Kanze Motomasa
teaching his son.

90. *Kanze Motomasa conducting a rehearsal*

91. Kanze Motomasa studying writings of his predecessors

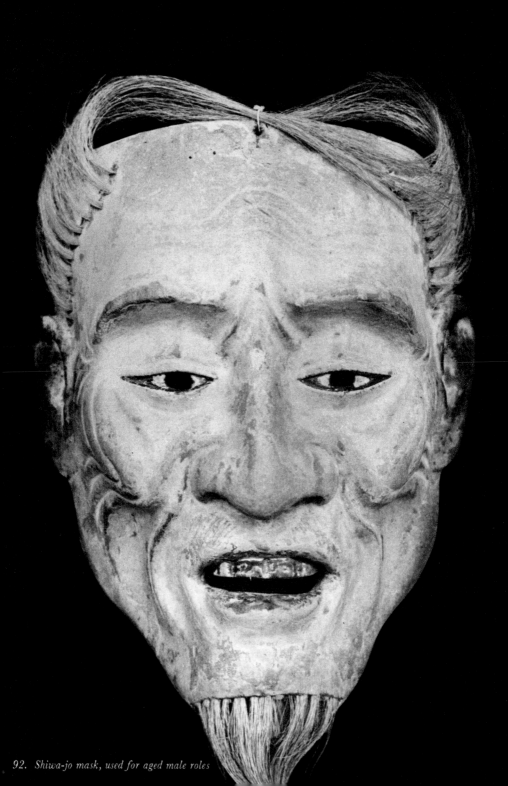

92. *Shiwa-jo mask, used for aged male roles*

93. *Sho-jo mask, used for aged male roles*

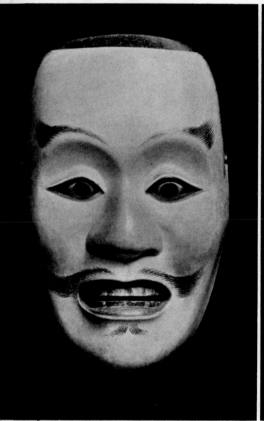

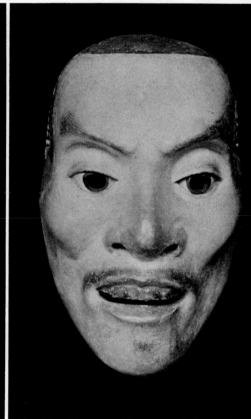

94. *Heida mask, used for warrior-ghost roles*   95. *Kaishi mask, used for ghost roles*

96. Otobide mask, used for demon roles   *97. Obeshimi mask, used for demon roles*

98. *Zo-onna mask, used for roles of beautiful middle-aged women*

99. Ko-omote mask, used for roles of beautiful young women

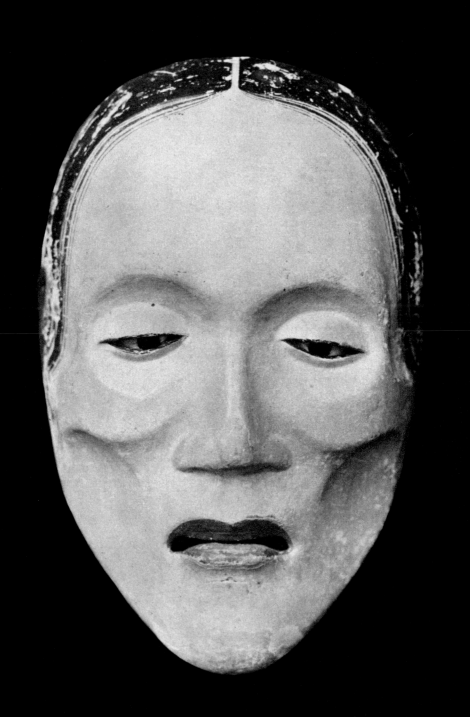

100. *Yase-onna mask, used for middle-aged female roles*

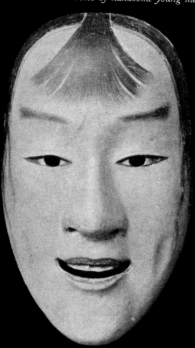

101. *Kasshiki mask, used for roles of handsome young men*

102. *Shintai mask, used for god roles*

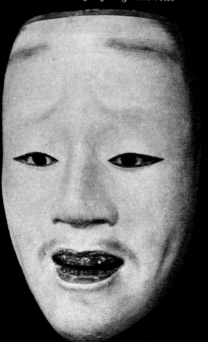

103. *Imawaka mask, used for young male roles*

104. *Shunkan mask, used only for the role of Shunkan*

105. *Hannya mask, used for ghosts of jealous women*

106. *Shikami mask, used for roles of angry ghosts*

107. *Shishi-guchi mask, used for lion roles* ▷

108. Brocade costume called karaori

109. Jacketlike brocade costume called kariginu

110. Cloaklike garment called suo

112. Trouserlike garment called hangiri

113. Cloaklike garment called happi

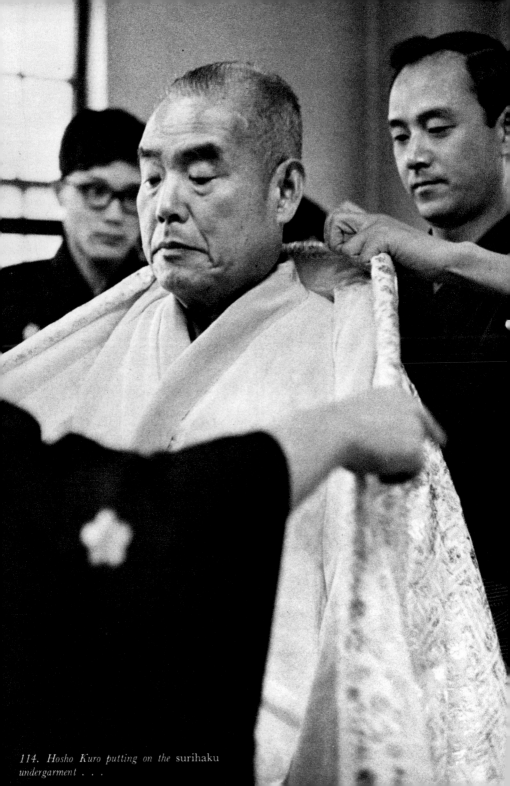

114. Hosho Kuro putting on the surihaku undergarment . . .

115. Putting on the nuihaku outer garment . . .

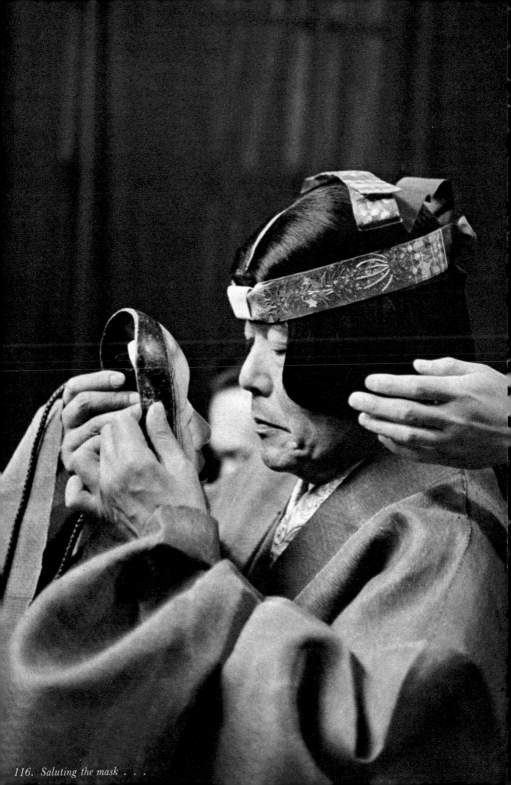

116. *Saluting the mask . . .*

117. *Contemplating his appearance . . .*

118. *At the stage entrance* . . . .

119. *On stage*

120. Modern Noh stage in the Kanze Noh Theater, Tokyo

121. *Sixteenth-century Noh stage at Nishi Hongan-ji, Kyoto*

122. *Thatched hut used in* Semimaru 123. *Shrine used in* Yokihi

124. *Mountain used in Momiji-gari*   125. *Thatched hut used in* Kagekiyo

126. *Prison used in* Rodaiko

127. *Palanquin used in* Nonomiya

128. *Boat used in* Eguchi

129. *Bell tower used in* Mii-dera   130. *Salt-gathering cart used in* Matsukaze

131. *Fulling block used in* Kinuta

32. *Bell used in* Dojo-ji

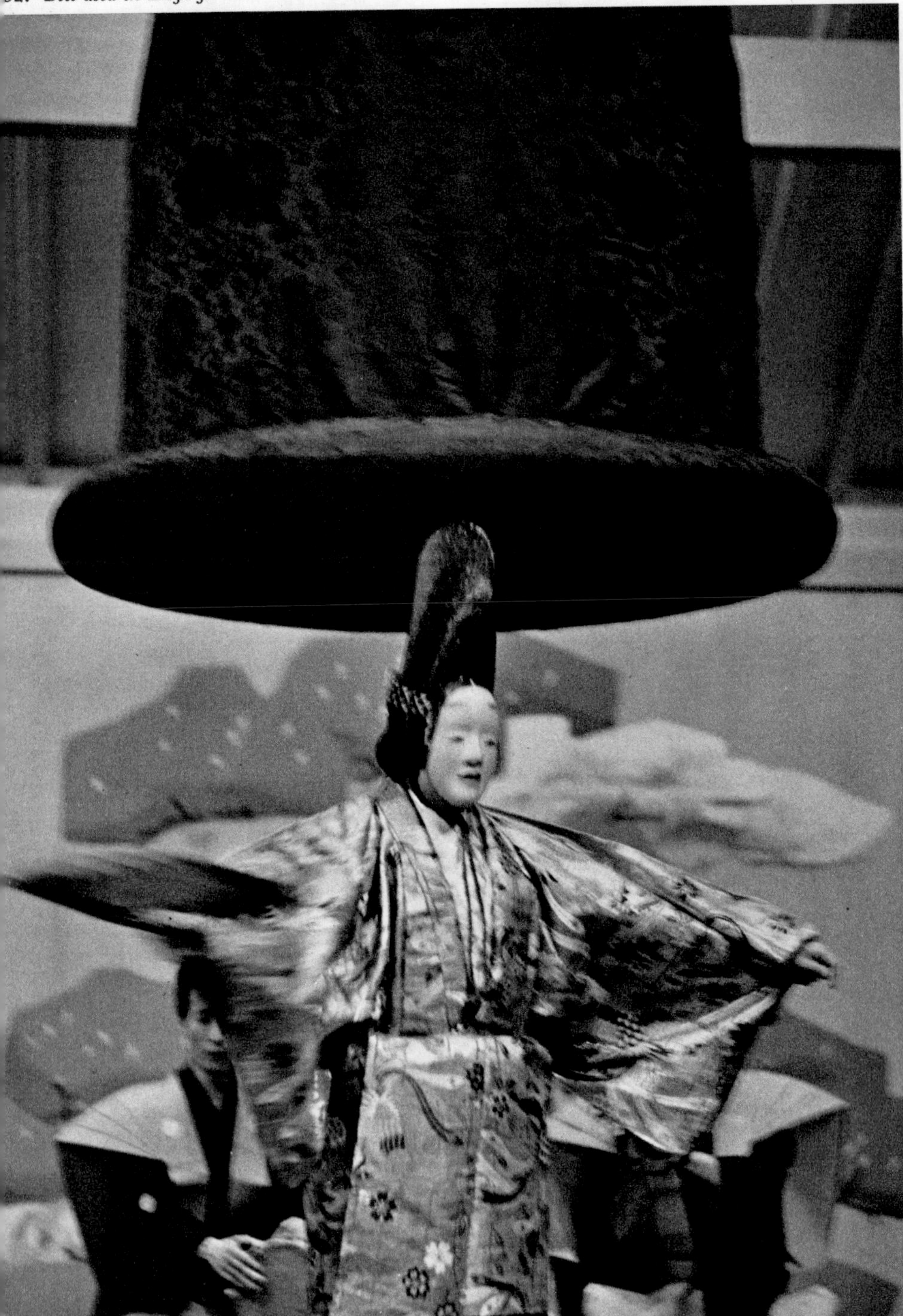

133. Drum stand used in Tenko

134. Yoke and water buckets used in Genj

135. Spinning wheel used in Kurozuka

136. Kane-no-ogi: *listening*

137. Tsuki-no-ogi: *moon viewing*

138. Hane-ogi: *flower viewing*

139. Another hane-ogi *movement*

140. Shikake: *a dance movement*

141. Hiraki: *a dance movement*

142. Makura-no-ogi: *sleeping*

143. Agehane: *a dance movement*

144. Kamae: *the basic pose*

145. Gassho: *praying or pleading*

146. Ashibyoshi: *heavy footbeats*

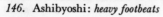

147. Hakobi: *a gliding walk*

148. Ryo-shiori: *deep sorrow*

149. Kata-shiori: *weeping*

150. Naginata: *describing battles*

151. Maki-sode: *great elation*

152–53. *Mask carver Irie Miho at work*

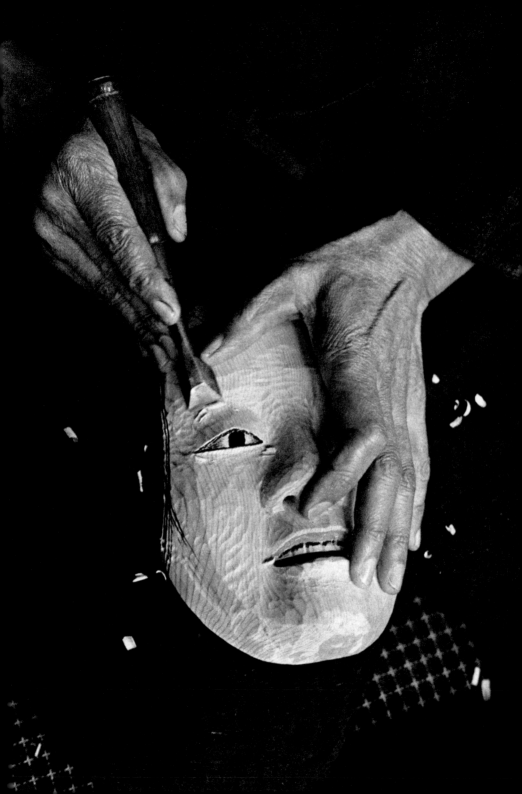

154–55. *Weaving cloth for Noh costumes*

158. Festival Noh: a performance of Ataka *in a proscenium theater*

159. Scene from Fukkatsu, *a modern Noh play*

160. *Scene from* Tsuru, *a modern Noh play*

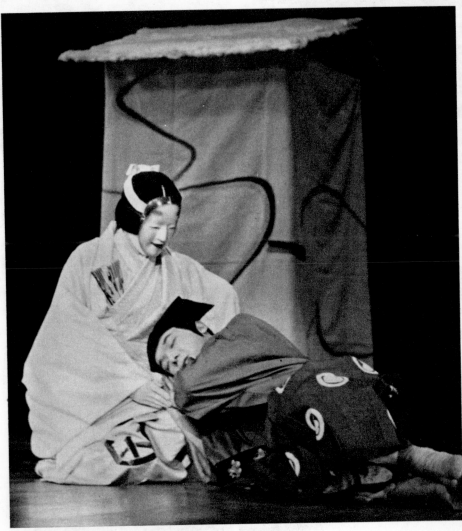

161. Scene from Yuzuru, *a modern Noh play*

loose jacket (*choken*) of light blue and purple covered with a design of chrysanthemums. Both the colors and the design of the garment add to the seasonal effect created by the Hyakuman costume (Plate 117). The *choken* is worn by most female characters who dance. It is a beautiful garment made of a stiff silk gauze in white or such shades as purple, blue, and pale green, decorated with gold-thread embroidery, and fastened in front with a long thick red cord tied in large hanging loops. The same kind of red cord is threaded around the edges of the broad sleeves and hangs in tassels from both sleeves, almost touching the ground (Plate 81). When the woman portrayed is a noblewoman of great dignity, the *nuihaku* is actually put on rather than draped from the waist in *koshimaki* style, and a broad stiff red trouserlike garment called the *okuchi* is worn under the *choken*. The *nuihaku* in *koshimaki* style is used in *Hyakuman*, *Matsukaze*, and *Futari Shizuka*, while the *nuihaku* with the *okuchi* is used for the roles of Izumi Shikibu in *Toboku*, Princess Rokujo in *Nonomiya*, and Imperial Princess Shokushi in *Teika*.

Of course along with these costumes the color and pattern of the sash and wig band are very carefully chosen to add to the total effect. Also the color of the collar band of the undergarment plays a very important part. Only the edge of it can be seen, but it tells the social rank of the character. There are both one-layer and two-layer collar bands. For female characters the colors are white, red, and light blue. White expresses the highest quality and red the lowest. Also the larger the number, the greater the dignity of the character. Hyakuman wears one collar band of the medium-quality color light blue.

The actor does not dress himself but is dressed very carefully by his fellow actors. During the Edo period there were specialists called *monogiseshi* who were responsible for dressing the actor.

Noh costumes seen on the stage today are exquisitely elegant, but this is a far cry from costumes seen on the stage in the early days of Sarugaku. In the book called *Lectures on Sarugaku* (Sarugaku Dangi) directions concerning the costumes for *Okina* state that "they should not be showy, but should be genteel—gold brocades and such should not be used." Also when the plain silk costumes used at the Kasuga Shrine are considered, we can imagine that they must have seemed the height of simplicity in comparison with the gorgeous Dengaku costumes used at the time the above book was written. Later, however, during On'ami's time, the costumes given to the actors by their sponsors for ceremonial and subscription performances of Sarugaku were generally made of gold brocades and silk damasks.

Originally, Noh costumes did not have the special unusual effect they have when seen today. Up through the Muromachi period they were similar to the clothing worn by the people of the times, and it was only during the Momoyama period that they began to take on the individual quality of stylized costumes.

Gekan Shoshin, a contemporary of Hideyoshi, in his book entitled *Dobu Sho,* mentions parts of the typical Noh costumes still used today, including such outer decorative garments as the *kariginu* (Plate 109), the *choken* (Plate 81), the *happi* (Plate 113), and the *hangiri* (Plate 112), as well as the basic kimono-shaped *karaori* (Plate 82), *nuihaku,* and *surihaku.* He gives measurements and instructions for making these garments. In his book *Soden Sho,* he says, "The sleeves should be cut especially broad to show off well the movements of the arms. If this is done, the total effect will be greatly heightened. The greatest of care should be taken in making female costumes." Here Shoshin indicated that the sleeves in everyday clothing, which until this time had been quite narrow (Plate 111), should be broadened for Noh costumes. Also around this time there developed the idea that no matter how poor the beggar, how deranged the woman, or how long the character portrayed may have been traveling, the costumes must never be realistically dirty or torn but must always express a refined beauty. Thus the sense of beauty for beauty's sake was introduced on the stage. Shoshin also gives attention to the interpretation of colors: "The color of the *kariginu* indicates rank. Red and blue should be used for higher ranks, yellow and black for lower ranks." In another book of the time, the phrase "music to match the color" appears—an indication that the attitude toward costumes had begun to resemble the attitude toward masks.

Around the beginning of the Edo period, the tendency to consider certain patterns and colors absolutely necessary for certain characters began to grow. With further advances in weaving and dyeing techniques, along with the support and patronage Noh received from the government during the Edo period, the unique beauty and refined taste evident in Noh costumes today was developed and formalized. Most of the costumes in use today were made during the Edo period.

From Dressing Room to Stage

PREPARATIONS HAVE BEEN COMPLETED in the dressing room for a performance of *Hyakuman,* and the actor moves to the greenroom (*kagami-no-ma;* literally, "mirror room"), the space behind the curtain at the end of the bridgelike passageway leading to the stage proper. The musicians play a short prelude backstage, indicating that it is almost time for the curtain to rise. In the greenroom there is a huge mirror in front of which the actor can contemplate his own appearance. The actor sits on a stool for some time, quietly studying his reflection. Finally he signals his assistant, the *koken,* who presents the mask. The actor makes a gesture of salutation to the mask (Plate 116), after which he places it on his face and the *koken* ties the strings firmly. This completes the costume. The actor's attitude toward the mask is aptly expressed in the admonition, "The mask is not put on the face, but the face should be thought of as being pulled into and clinging to the mask." The atmosphere in the greenroom becomes tense as the actor quietly waits for his entrance cue in front of the mirror (Plate 117). At this point he has already entered the *yugen* of the play to be performed. He moves to his position just behind the curtain. In his hand is the bamboo branch (*sasa*) which symbolizes the deranged state of Hyakuman's mind. The attitude and stance of the actor when he takes his position here is very important. The distance he stands from the curtain differs according to the role. In the case of Hyakuman, who is searching for her lost child, a sense of eagerness is expressed by standing very close to the curtain.

The *shite* listens to the singing of the *ai-kyogen,* who is performing the *dainembutsu* dance, till he hears his cue. Then he whispers, "O-maku" (the curtain). Two *koken* raise the curtain. The appearance of the *shite* has been described as similar to a famous painting by the Chinese artist Liang K'ai depicting the descent of Sakyamuni (the Buddha) from the mountain immediately after his enlightenment. The comparison is appropriate because the proper state of mind for a *shite* is the total emptying of all thoughts and feelings from the mind and complete concentration like the state required for Buddhist enlightenment. In his treatise *Six Blossoms and One Drop of Dew* (Rikurin Ichiro; Plate 63), Komparu Zenchiku, who was especially influenced by Zen Buddhism, divides the performance of a play into six levels, beginning with the entrance and ending with the exit of the *shite.* He explains that the six blossoms (that is, levels), when brought to full bloom, make up the spiritual single drop of dew which is the essence of the *shite's* art. In this way Noh and Zen have been brought together in their search for all in nothingness. The first glimpse of the *shite* as he appears (Plate 118) is the most exciting moment of the play for Noh enthusiasts, who can instantly determine his intended interpretation of the role by the mask and costume he has chosen.

Hyakuman stops on the *hashigakari* for a time and stares at the *ai-kyogen* as he moves in his dance. Then she advances with swift whispering footsteps and strikes him on the shoulder with her bamboo branch. She begins the *mondo* (conversation) with the *ai-kyogen:* "The rhythm of your dance had drawn me to this place. I must dance with you." She proceeds to the *joza* (upstage right) and begins reciting the Buddhist prayer "Namu Amida Butsu." The chorus repeats it after her and continues to sing, describing a person in the rain on a moonlit night. Hyakuman proceeds a few steps in the direction of the *shosaki* (downstage center) position and looks toward the moon in the western sky, then performs the *sayu* (described in the later section entitled "Stage Movement") while singing, "The skies do not clear, but I continue toward the west . . . always searching for someone." She goes all the way to the *shosaki* (downstage center) and begins singing the *issei*—in this case a song about pulling a cart heavily loaded with sorrows—using the bamboo branch in mimed movement. The chorus takes up the song while Hyakuman continues to dance, proceeding first to the *shochu* (center stage), where she points left and right, circles to the left, and once more does a *sayu* when she reaches the *daishomae* (upstage center). This is the *kuruma-no-dan* (literally, "cart-pulling scene"), which reveals her suffering heart and deranged mind. The chorus continues singing, and the *sasa-no-dan* (bamboo-branch scene) begins. This scene is a dance describing the mother's love for her lost son, through vigorous movements in all directions. It ends when she folds her hands at the *shosaki* (downstage center) and prays that she will be allowed to see her son once more.

The space within which the *shite* may move includes of course the whole stage and the *hashigakari*. The *hashigakari* is not simply a passageway to connect the dressing room and the stage. In the case of *Hyakuman* the *shite* utilizes the *hashigakari* by stopping there for a time to watch the dance of the *ai-kyogen*. This of course is a use of the *hashigakari* as an extension of the stage. The four pillars setting off the area of the stage itself are important points of reference for the action of the actors. When viewed from the audience, the pillar nearest the *hashigakari* at the back of the stage is the *shite-bashira*, the one opposite it to the right is called the *fue-bashira* because of its proximity to the flutist's (*fue-kata*) seat. The pillar at the front of the stage on the right is next to the position generally taken by the *waki* and thus is called the *waki-bashira*, while the one on the left-front corner of the stage is called the *metsuke-bashira*, meaning "the pillar on which to place the eyes." This pillar is used as a guidepost for all movement on the stage. The position just to the right of the *shite-bashira* is called the *joza*. This is where the *shite* stops and makes his first statement when he enters the main stage area. Most of the actions of the *shite* originate and end at this point. The position called *daishomae* is just in front of the position of the *otsuzumi* and *kotsuzumi* (large hand drum and small hand drum) players—in other words, upstage center. *Shosaki* is the point closest to the audience at downstage center, and *shochu* is in the very center of the stage. Also there are positions designated *waki-za* (position of the *waki* near the *waki-bashira*), *jiutai-mae* (in front of the chorus), *fueza-mae* (in front of the flutist), *wakisho* (between the *shite-bashira* and *metsuke-bashira*), and *kokenza* (position of the *koken* at the farthest point upstage to the left, directly behind the *joza*). These positions are used in the notation of choreography and stage blocking. Of course the designations came into being along with the formalization of the art itself, but they must have been developed somewhat later than the early stylization of movement, since none of them are mentioned in the early work on notation called *Dobu Sho*. As part of the standardization process that began when Noh became the official property of the Tokugawa shogunate, the Noh stage also became standardized. This development took place about the middle of the Edo period, and the Noh stage built inside Edo Castle served as the model. The terms designating the various areas and positions on the stage came into use and were codified after the building of the Edo Castle stage and others that followed the same specifications.

Recently, in answer to complaints that movement on the traditional Noh stage cannot be fully viewed because of the *metsuke-bashira*, stages have been built without this pillar—especially in theaters which are commonly used for other purposes and in which the Noh stage is a temporary structure placed on the floor of a regular proscenium stage. The traditional Noh stage protrudes out into the audience—a custom left over from the early forms of Noh, which were basically for ritual purposes rather than for entertainment. The *metsuke-bashira* was a necessary feature for support of the roofs of the temples and shrines where these ceremonies took place. Even though Noh has completely lost its ceremonial aspects and the actors can easily perform without the aid of this pillar, it still holds a very important position in creating the unique space of Noh. No matter how carefully the other specifications of the stage are copied in these new stages without *metsuke-bashira*, the three-dimensional space effect peculiar to the traditional stage is almost completely lost. Without the *metsuke-bashira* the distance between the audience and an actor moving in the area close to the *metsuke-bashira* cannot be clearly established, and the consequent loss of a feeling of depth makes the whole play seem both literally and figuratively flat and lifeless.

As we have noted before, the traditional stage as it exists today has come down to us from the Momoyama period. Before that time Sarugaku was performed in whatever space was available: sanctuaries, ritual stages of temples and shrines, or even on a marked-out space on the ground. The firelight (*takigi*) Noh at the Kofuku-ji is performed on a low platform placed on the ground, and that of the Wakamiya Festival at the Kasuga Shrine is performed on a similar temporary platform (originally performed on the surface of the ground itself) at the foot of the Yogo Pine. The subscription Noh performances, even in Zeami's day, were given on hastily constructed platforms surrounded by straw mats spread on the ground for the audience to sit on. These stages were so poorly constructed that the actors always inspected them before performing, insisting that protruding nails and other defects which seemed dangerous be corrected. In these early days, the *hashigakari* extended directly back from the very center of the stage. It was moved to its present position at the side of the stage between 1504 and 1521. This change was designed to facilitate the viewing of Noh from a parlor-type room across a gravel area in front of the stage. At the same time a painting of a huge pine tree was placed at the back of the stage and called, as it is today, the *kagami-ita* (literally, "mirror board"). This is the only object on the Noh stage which can be considered "decorative." The painted pine tree, which has almost become the very symbol of Noh today, was originally placed there to represent the Yogo Pine of the Kasuga Shrine. It has been believed from ancient days in Japan that the gods reside in the pine tree. At any rate, compared with other types of stages, there is none as simple in design as the Noh stage. This almost completely sceneryless stage goes very well with the symbolic aspects of the art of Noh.

Noh consists entirely of song, rhythm, and the simple stylized movements of the actor. For instance, the *shite* in *Hyakuman* performs a dance while singing, "I pass through the evening dew of Ogura village in Matsuo. My sleeves are drenched with tears of sorrow. I peer through robes of flowers and finally reach this temple where all souls come to seek rest." The dance movement consists simply of circling from downstage center to the right as far as the *joza*, proceeding forward to the *metsuke-bashira*, where the opened fan is raised above the head as though shading the eyes, once more circling to the right while pointing straight ahead with the fan, and looking into the distance when reaching downstage center while still pointing in the same direction with the fan. These extremely abstract movements accompanied by chanting and rhythms must be absolutely incomprehensible to one who is viewing Noh for the first time with no foreknowledge of the art. But when the dramatic power and concentration of the actor touches the heart of the informed sensitive spectator, he is seized by the deep grief in the heart of Hyakuman. On this bare stage he senses the evening dew of Saga. This is possible in Noh precisely because there are no unnecessary objects to distract the imagination.

Stage Properties

OCCASIONALLY SCENERY-LIKE OBJECTS called *tsukuri-mono* (Plates 122–35) are used on the Noh stage. The *tsukuri-mono* are abstractions which may represent a mountain, a mound, a grove of trees, a small shrine or temple, a thatched hut, a cart or a wagon, a boat, a well, or a *torii* (the entrance gate to a shrine).

These objects are made of bamboo poles wrapped in narrow strips of white cloth and sometimes embellished with branches of trees or artificial flowers. A platform about three by six feet and about one foot high covered with cloth is often used to represent a throne, a dance stage, or a bridge. When decorated with a canopy, trees, or sacred straw ropes, it can represent a sanctuary, a palace, or a swordsmith's forge. There are also other smaller stage props, including a salt gatherer's cart, a spinning wheel, a fulling block, a drum stand, a mirror stand, a creel, a bundle of brushwood, a pole, a broom, a twig, a bamboo branch, and a cane. Hand props include straw hats, umbrellas, fans, Buddhist rosaries, mirrors, letters, poem cards, swords, daggers, long swords, halberds, drums, small hand gongs, and incense. The *tsukuri-mono* are all striking masterpieces of economy which harmonize well with the simplicity of the stage itself. This simplicity provides a contrast with the subtly expressive masks and the gorgeous costumes, making the actor stand out in sharp relief. The *tsukuri-mono* are important in the action of some plays. For instance, the grove of trees in *Arashi-yama* and the bridge in *Shakkyo* stress the location where the action takes place. The palanquin in *Yuya* and the boat in *Funa Benkei* make the scene changes very impressive. Other *tsukuri-mono* serve to intensify the emotional atmosphere at the climax of a piece—for instance, when the *shite* looks into the well in *Izutsu* and sees reflected there the face of her dead lover Narihira, or when the *shite* of *Kinuta*, while beating on the fulling block, reminisces about her husband, who is away in a far country. In order to allow the actor to suddenly appear or disappear at the very center of the stage, sometimes a frame completely covered by a curtain of damask is set in the center of the stage. In some cases the actor enters this enclosure before it is brought on the stage, and in others he disappears into it during the progress of the play. In Tokugawa times there were specialists attached to each troupe whose job it was to construct these stage props, but today they are made by the actors themselves.

Among the hand props, the folding fan, or *ogi*, has a unique position. All the actors, the musicians, and the chorus carry fans. There are two kinds of fans, the common *ogi* and the *chukei*. The *chukei*, when folded, looks like a leaf of the maidenhair tree. Almost all *shite* and *waki* carry a *chukei* when they appear on the stage. There are many different *ogi* styles, each designated for the type of character for which it is used (Plate 84). The Okina fan has a picture of Mount Horai, the Jo fan an ink painting of the seven Chinese wise men, the god fan a paulownia tree and phoenixes, the ghost fan waves and the rising sun, the woman or wig fan a flower palanquin, the old-woman fan a bridge and herons, and the demon fan a single large peony blossom. Hyakuman carries the madwoman fan, which pictures a pine tree and clematis blossoms.

The common *ogi* has the special pattern of the school in which it is used and is carried by all participants in a performance except the *shite* and *waki*. It is also used when *utai* and dance are performed without costumes in the forms called *su utai* and *su mai*, in which case the formal black kimono and *hakama* (skirtlike trousers) are worn.

Hyakuman uses very few stage or hand props. The *shite* carries only the bamboo branch which symbolizes a deranged mind. This slender branch, cut from the variety of bamboo which has a solid rather than a hollow stem, is the same as those which have always been used by shrine maidens in their dances as a symbol of divine inspiration. The deranged mother searching for her lost child in a Noh drama has a degree of divine inspiration in that the minute she sees her child again she is cured.

After about an hour of performance time, Hyakuman reaches

the part called the *kiri*, in which the mother and child meet and express their joy at being reunited as they return to the capital. The capital is reached and the play is finished when they come to the *joza* and perform the final foot beats called *tome-byoshi*. The *shite* then passes quietly along the *hashigakari* and disappears behind the curtain. He removes the mask and salutes it once more, then resumes his own individuality. He sits in the center of the greenroom and thanks each of the actors and musicians as they leave the stage and enter the greenroom.

The question is often asked whether a Noh play ends when the *shite* performs the final *tome-byoshi* at the *joza* or when he has passed through the *hashigakari* and entered the greenroom. The modern way of thinking seems to deem it natural to applaud as the *shite* retreats along the *hashigakari*. There are even some who have the disagreeable habit of breaking into applause the second the *tome-byoshi* has been performed. Zenchiku insisted that the acting of a piece is not completed till the *shite* actually enters the greenroom. The opportunity to enjoy the afterglow of a piece by silently viewing the actor as he slowly retreats along the *hashigakari* in character can be enjoyed in no other form of drama. The afterglow of a well-performed Noh play should last longer than these few seconds. Thus our last impression as we watch Hyakuman return to a world different from our own is very important. This transition should be understood and appreciated in contemplative silence.

Music

THE APPEARANCE OF THE SHITE on the stage takes place after the *waki*, *tsure*, and others have made their entrances, in some cases while they are singing and in other cases in response to the call of one of them. However, no matter what form the cue takes, the *shite's* entrance is almost always accompanied by the *hayashi* orchestra. The *hayashi* music is often described as *shibyoshi* (literally, "four beat"), but this term refers not to the music itself but to the four instruments which make up the orchestra: flute, *kotsuzumi* or small hand drum, *otsuzumi* or large hand drum, and *taiko* or floor drum (Plate 83). The rather showy aspect of the *taiko* limits its use to a certain extent. It does not always appear on the stage, but the other three are always used. These musical instruments, in comparison with those of the West, are extremely simple in design, and the sounds they produce are equally simple. This simplicity serves to strengthen the unique symbolism of Noh, which demands a rich imagination on the part of the viewer. In spite of the seeming simplicity of the sounds, the training of the musicians is very strict, and they go to great pains to set the proper mood and create a background appropriate to each play and character.

There are two main types of entrance music for the entrance of the *waki* and the *shite* in the first half of a play. They are called *shidai* and *issei*. Both are songs accompanied by the *kotsuzumi*, the *otsuzumi*, and the flute. More than likely the average viewer cannot at first differentiate between these two styles, but if one listens carefully the difference gradually becomes evident. The *issei* is more rhythmical than the *shidai*. It is full of emotion and is sung on the beat. The *shidai* is not sung on the beat. Even so, this does not mean that the *shidai* is any less powerful; it is simply not as rhythmical. Each single beat is just as full of vigorous spirit as the more rhythmical *issei*. At present, at most performances attended by people who are supposed to know Noh well, the entrance music is performed amidst the noise of gossiping voices and latecomers bustling to their seats. This is a regrettable situation. Those who really wish to experience Noh should be sitting quietly in anticipation of the first glimpse and the first utterance of the *shite*, whose whole mind and soul are concentrated on this first moment.

There are two different styles of *issei:* the "true *issei*" and the "common *issei*." Also the *issei* which introduces the *shite* of the second part of a play is different in quality and feeling, depending on the type of character to appear. Just as the mask and costume are chosen with great care, the *hayashi* (Noh music) is chosen to create an image of the character in the mind of the viewer before the curtain is raised to reveal the costumed actor. There are several varieties of *hayashi*, such as the *dewa* and the *hayabue*, which are used for gods, dragons, ghosts of men and women, demons and beasts, personifications by foxes, and so forth; the *obeshi*, used for the long-nosed demons called *tengu;* and the *sagariha,* used for angels.

Hayashi is of course used not only as entrance music but as accompaniment to the *utai* as well. There are two kinds of *utai*, referred to as *tsuyogin* (literally, "strong chant") and *yowagin* (literally, "weak chant"). This does not indicate a difference in pitch or key but in the actual use of the voice. *Yowagin* is quite similar to Western singing, but *tsuyogin* is found only in Noh. *Yowagin* is full of curving lines while *tsuyogin* is very angular. In other words, *yowagin* is a lyrical form of expression, while *tsuyogin* is more appropriate for expressing heroic and majestic themes. Zeami, in his *Treatise on Music and the Use of the Voice* (Ongyoku Kowadashi Kuden) divides the types of voice into the "congratulatory voice," which is exhilarating and bright, with no dark shadows, and the "pathetic voice," which is refined and graceful, with a weird beauty and full of dark, sighing shadows. *Hyakuman* is of the *yowagin* ("pathetic voice") variety, along with all other *yugen*-type woman (wig) pieces. Most *waki* Noh use *tsuyogin* ("congratulatory voice"), which perfectly

characterizes their congratulatory atmosphere. This differ-
entiation became extremely exaggerated in importance when
su utai first gained its great popularity. The terms *tsuyogin* and
yowagin began to appear in the *utai-bon* during the first part of
the Edo period, but it was not until the Meiji era that they
came into general use and were more or less officially recognized
by the schools of Noh.

The third responsibility of the *hayashi-kata* is the accompaniment of the dances. Dance holds such an important position in
Noh that it is used at the climax of almost every piece.

One more important element which affects the whole of the
art of Noh is the *jo-ha-kyu* theory. The movement patterns (*kata*,
which are discussed in the next section) of Noh control space,
but time is controlled by *jo-ha-kyu*. This is a traditional mode
which originated in Bugaku and also played an important role
in the poetry form called *renga*. Zeami explained *jo-ha-kyu* in the
following way in *The Flower Mirror* (Kakyo): "*Jo* is the beginning, therefore the most correct, the most basic natı ral
figure. *Ha* breaks into and harmonizes with *jo* and presents a
detailed exposition of it. *Kyu* is the final embellishment in which
all is brought to a close with complicated, fast, vigorous movement." All expressions of time transition in Noh, including the
structure of the play, the *hayashi* accompaniment, the dance
movement, and the *utai*, are governed by *jo-ha-kyu*.

Stage Movement

HYAKUMAN IS ONE OF THE OLDEST Noh pieces, and thus the mime
element in it is strong. Each *kata* (movement pattern) of the
shite is a movement which illustrates the lyrics of the *utai*. This
is especially true of the movement patterns in the previously

described *kuruma-no-dan* and *sasa-no-dan*. Words such as "look toward the west," "pull the cart," *sashi, sashi-mawashi, sayu, gassho,* and *sashi-wake* are used to describe these movement patterns. Each is the name of a *kata* which designates the movement to be made by the actor. *Sashi* means to move the fan held in the right hand from the right side to directly above the head, then down to a position straight out in front of the chest, as though pointing to something far in the distance. *Sashi-mawashi* begins with the fan pointed straight forward in front of the chest. Next the actor takes two steps backward, beginning with the left foot, then turns to the right while spreading the right arm out to a forty-five-degree angle. When one rotation is completed, he takes two steps forward, beginning with the right foot. *Sashi-wake* consists of performing the *sashi-mawashi* first to the left, then to the right. *Sayu* means to point to the left at a forty-five-degree angle and take two steps in that direction, beginning with the left foot, then point to the right at a forty-five-degree angle and take two steps in that direction beginning with the right foot. *Gassho* means to lightly place the hands together in front of and slightly below the face in an attitude of prayer. The *gassho* is easily understood as prayer, but none of the others have any intrinsic meaning, so that when viewed separately they seem to express nothing. Often the lyrics sung when they are performed lend them meaning, but there are also times when they seem to have no relationship to the meaning of the piece in which they appear.

All together there are more than two hundred *kata* used in Noh today. The separate *kata* and their names are necessary for the actor in his training and memorization of choreography, but a knowledge of them is not necessary in the viewing and appreciation of Noh. The fact is that *kata* did not exist during the early days of Noh in their present set form but began to appear as Noh became refined and formalized. As a result, even the *kata* with strong mime elements do not employ everyday natural gestures but are highly stylized suggestions of them. For instance in the *shiori*, which depicts weeping, the actor simply bows his head slightly and raises his hand (which is held flat with the palm facing upward at an oblique angle) to a position in front of his eyes. He never sniffles or trembles as in realistic crying.

Even in cases where extreme grief is to be expressed, he only raises both hands instead of one. It is said that in Zeami's time some actors actually wiped their eyes with their sleeves when showing grief. Zeami advised that a truly skillful actor should never resort to this type of realistic action, but it seems to have been common practice in his day. This shows just how stylized today's *kata* have become. There are even times when the *shite* does nothing but sit still in the middle of the stage with his head bowed slightly while the chorus sings of his deep sorrow. This highly stylized *kata* is called *iguse*. To the uninitiated it probably appears to be extremely boring and to require no skill whatsoever to perform, but the fact is that if the actor is not highly disciplined, he cannot maintain the concentration necessary for the "action in silence" (*seichu-no-do*) which this *kata* demands.

The dance forms of Noh originated in the Shinto *kagura* dances, which were steeped in ceremony and etiquette, since they were from the beginning a presentation expressing reverence toward a being of higher position than the performer. The fan which is always carried by all those who appear on the stage in Noh is a holdover from this traditional etiquette. Since the *kata* are for the most part artistic stylizations of ancient etiquette, some persons even go to the extent of referring to Noh as the "fan art."

A closer look at the *kata* shows that each is made up of a *kamae* (pose or posture) and a *hakobi* (progression). Whether it is a standing or a sitting *kamae,* there must never be any sign of relaxation in any part of the body. In other words, the actor must concentrate every part of his body and all his senses on the *kamae* in order to fully express the character he is playing. The *hakobi* is basically the progression in space achieved by the unique style of walking in which the heel is always in contact with the floor. Only the toes rise off the floor as the feet slide whispering along the smooth boards of the stage. The effect should be that of the whole body held firmly in a sculptural pose while slipping along lightly and smoothly. This is "silence in action" (*dochu-no-sei*), as opposed to the "action in silence" of the *iguse* described above, which, combined with a sense of rhythm and a sensitive interpretation, creates the *kamae* and *hakobi* appropriate to each *kata*. The traditional snow-white *tabi* socks always worn in Noh greatly strengthen the impression of the movement of the feet. The absolute unity of the *kata,* whether they be meaningful as mime or purely abstract, is never lacking in total harmony.

As we have noted earlier, the beautifully stylized movement patterns of Noh were not created in a day. During the centuries of its development, Noh was influenced first by Zen Buddhist culture and later by the strict warrior cult of the Tokugawa period as it moved along the road toward perfection. The various *kata* thus perfected over the centuries must be mastered by the actor to the extent that his body unconsciously tenses and takes the proper pose to form the *kata* required when he is on the stage. Each school has its own slight variations in the *kata*. Generally speaking, the basic differences lie in the tendency of the Kanze and Hosho schools to concentrate on details producing a neat and sharp, smaller effect, while the Komparu, Kongo, and Kita schools are more fond of broad dramatic poses which produce a larger effect.

In *The Flower Mirror* Zeami made an interesting comment on the relationship between physical and mental movement: "When I say to set the mind in action at full capacity while moving the body at only seven-tenths of capacity, I mean that the body should be moved by using the arms and legs just as the master teaches. Then, after you have polished and perfected what you have learned, you should perform by using all the powers of your mind and heart while moving your body with the greatest possible economy. This is true not only in dance but also in all movements executed during the time one is on the stage. The body should at all times be working much less than the heart and mind. The body performs the piece itself while the true substance of the play is expressed from the inner depths of the heart and mind. In this way you will be able to hold the interest of your audience."

Noh Today and in the Future

SINCE THE DAYS OF ZEAMI, some six hundred years ago, the spring of Noh has never gone dry. Noh is not of value simply because it is old. It is of value because of the fact that through the six hundred years of its existence it has always maintained a hold on the hearts of the people and has continued to communicate with them. Noh is not so difficult to understand and appreciate. It is just that today it has come to be considered a classic form (the word itself seems to most people to connote something mystic and hard to understand) and efforts have been made to preserve its abstract forms. There seems to be no interest whatsoever in reviving the original forms found in old drawings and pictures, which might give it new freshness and vigor. The performers think only of mastering and passing on the traditional techniques, and those who view the performance look only for these same techniques. Thus it has come to be believed that no one except those who are taking lessons in dance or *utai* can understand a Noh performance. The way to really appreciate Noh is to see with the eyes and feel with the heart, thus communicating with the heart of the actor. Anyone who comes with an open and receptive mind can gain something of the deep aspects of Noh from a good performance. "True art should not be understood, but experienced." The most important point in the appreciation of any form of art is expressed in these words. That which is seen should be allowed to lead one to the unseen inner depths expressed there.

Since Noh is basically performed in absolutely the same way every time, according to formalized scripts and set choreography, it is often referred to as a regenerative art. But it is a problem whether or not, by watching a performance today, one can get the feel of Noh as it was in the Muromachi period. One can sense the period by viewing its painting, its sculpture, and its architecture, but Noh is another matter. As we have noted in reviewing its history, it went through many changes after the days of Kan'ami and Zeami until it was finally stylized in the Edo period. But even after strict stylization took over, changes continued.

Zeami taught that Noh must appeal to the audience of the day and that too much time and effort should not be wasted on maintaining old worn-out traditions of the past. Even since the Meiji era changes have been made. A good example is the pose of the actor when he is performing the part of a beautiful woman. At present the feet are kept close together, but up to the Mejii era no particular care was taken, and the stance was decidedly masculine, with the feet a generous distance apart. This bringing of the feet together is a result of the influence of imported Western drama, which stresses realism. Thus the change was brought about, and we see the more feminine pose today. In this way changes are constantly being made even now. It is not true that there is absolutely no freedom in Noh today. As long as people live and the art continues to exist, even the set *utai* and *kata* find themselves being given new interpretations and new life. There is always the possibility for change and rebirth through the individual personality of the performer. These innovations are not made simply to destroy the old traditions but have the purpose of refining and deepening a living art. Even with the drastic changes that have been brought about through the years, the ideas that Kan'ami and Zeami taught can still be seen filling the Noh stage with life today. These precepts must not be forgotten when writing new Noh scripts (Plates 159, 160) or when using themes from Noh in newer theatrical forms (Plate 161).

The gorgeously brilliant Noh seen on the stages of Japan today is not without its problems. For instance, the Noh actors find it impossible to make a living through performances only. They must supplement their earnings by teaching *utai* and *shimai* (dance). The *shite* actors can get by this way, but the *waki* actors, the *hayashi* musicians, and the Kyogen actors have a difficult time of it because their students are few. There is every possibility that Noh will die out if some financial aid is not given it in the near future. First of all there should be substantial government support for Noh as a national art. There is a desperate need for a second Iwakura Tomomi, who would choose some of the younger performers who show promise and give them the necessary support to devote themselves wholly to the maintenance of the traditions of their art.

Noh was not originally created as symbolic drama, but it certainly has developed many symbolic aspects. For this reason it is possible to perform it as pure symbolic drama. This is the kind of interpretation that appeals to modern-day audiences. The old is unexpectedly new. Ionesco said, "Noh is avant-garde theater. . . . Modes of theatrical expression which are fine-textured and filled with mystery but have a condensed stylization like those of Japan can be found only in the Orient. It is into this utterly quiet lake of ancient wisdom which is the Orient that we wish to dip." Here Ionesco expresses the feeling of modern European dramatists that an impasse has been reached in the realm of expression on the stage and that Noh may be the key to further freedom and development. An Italian director said, "I saw something very basically theatrical in the simple, strong beauty of Noh." On the same occasion England's Dexter pointed out, "Western theatrical tradition is a history of expression through the use of dialogue, whereas the traditional structure of Oriental theater is made up of song, dance, and movement." In the stylized traditional modes of aesthetic and intellectual expression of Oriental theater these men have found the festival or ceremonial aspect which is, after all, the origin of all forms of theater. I believe that Noh also has a lot to offer in the field of dramaturgy.

At any rate, Noh is alive in the present world. It is a theatrical art of today. It stands up under the scrutiny of modern man. The problem of the form in which Noh should be passed on to future generations is one that must be seriously considered by performer and viewer alike. "Life will end, but Noh will never die." These words of Zeami echo down to us across the centuries.

Chronology

200 B.C. Song and dance formed a part of tribal ceremonies and festivals,
to about including funerals, harvest celebrations, building rites, etc. Tribal
A.D. 500 dances were performed in honor of the new lord when a tribe was
          conquered.

A.D. 612 Mimashi, a man from Kudara (a kingdom in Korea), became a
          Japanese citizen and introduced Gigaku to Japan.

698   Bugaku and Sangaku were brought in from China and became
          very popular.

701   Gagaku was adopted as the official music of the court.

743   Emperor Shomu composed a dance in the *gosechi-no-mai* style.

752   Bugaku and Sangaku were performed at the dedication ceremony
          of the Great Buddha at the temple called Todai-ji.

781   Gagaku was included for the first time in the emperor's first
          harvest festival, the Daijoe.

782   Dengaku actors, who had become a part of the official Gagaku
          troupe, were eliminated from the court.

1011   *The Tale of Genji* (Genji Monogatari) was written about this time
          by Murasaki Shikibu.

1018   Aristocrats began to perform the *ennen* dances.

1023   The regent Fujiwara Michinaga attended a performance of *taue*,
          the Dengaku dance for the rice-planting festival.

1040   Sangaku and *furyu* dances were performed at the Inari Festival.

1060   Fujiwara Akihira wrote the *Shin Sarugaku Ki*.

1096   Dengaku was extremely popular in Kyoto.

1136   Fujiwara Tadamichi, chief adviser to the emperor, initiated the
          Wakamiya Festival at the Kasuga Shrine. Sarugaku and Dengaku
          were both performed as part of this festival.

1141   Sangaku performed by priests called *shushi* was popular.

1150   Dengaku priest-actors began to appear and formed two groups
          called the Honza, meaning "original troupe," and the Shinza,
          meaning "new troupe."

1255   The first record of firelight (*takigi*) Noh is dated this year.

233

1283   There is a record of *ennen* as well as Chigo, Okina, Samba, Chichi-no-jo, and Emmei Kaja dances performed by priests at the Kofuku-ji, a temple in Nara, during this year. This is the earliest record of *Okina* performed in a formal style by Sarugaku actors.

1333   Kiyotsugu (better known as Kan'ami) was born.

1340   A performance of *ennen-furyu* dances was held at the Horyu-ji temple in Nara.

1349   Dengaku Noh and Sarugaku Noh were performed by Shinto priests and shrine maidens at the Kasuga Shrine. Ashikaga Takau-ji, the shogun, attended a performance of subscription Dengaku at Shijo-gawara in Kyoto. During this performance, the stalls broke down, and many of the spectators were injured. *Kuse-mai* dances and *kouta* songs were at the height of their popularity.

1363   Motokiyo (better known as Zeami) was born about this time.

1368   Kan'ami used a *kuse-mai* dance for the first time in a play called *Shirahige*.

1372   Kan'ami gained great popularity after a seven-day performance at the Daigo-ji temple.

1374   Kan'ami and his son Fujiwaka (Zeami's childhood name) performed the ceremonial Sarugaku at the Imakumano Shrine. Shogun Yoshimitsu attended this performance.

1378   Fujiwaka (Zeami) and Yoshimitsu attended the Gion Festival together and shared the same seat.

1381   Fujiwaka came of age and took the adult name Kanze Saburo Motokiyo. The Dengaku actor Itchu was popular at this time.

1384   Kan'ami performed his last Noh in what is now the city of Shizuo-ka and died nearby in Suruga. Motokiyo (Zeami) became the second head of the Kanze troupe.

1394   Motomasa, Motokiyo's first son, was born.

1396   Inuo, the Sarugaku actor from Omi, and his troupe were active in Kyoto about this time.

1398   Motoshige (On'ami) was born.

1399   Motokiyo (Zeami) performed a season of subscription Sarugaku in Kyoto which the shogun Yoshimitsu attended.

1400   Motokiyo wrote the first three chapters of *Fushi Kaden* (The Transmission of the Flower of the Art), which is more commonly known as the *Kadensho*.

1401   Motokiyo changed his name to Zeami.

1402   Zeami wrote the fourth, fifth, and sixth chapters of the *Kadensho*. It is thought that he also wrote *The Seventh Supplement to the Kadensho* (Kaden Dainana Besshi Kuden) during this year.

1405   Komparu Ujinobu (later known as Zenchiku) was born.

1408   Emperor Gokomatsu attended a performance by Inuo and his Dengaku troupe at Yoshimitsu's Kitayama Palace.

1411   Yoshimochi became shogun and gave his support and patronage to the Dengaku actor-priest Zoami. During the following ten years or so, annual subscription Dengaku performances held the attention of the court. Zeami and his Sarugaku became more and more a thing of the past.

1419   Zeami wrote his *Treatise on Music and the Use of the Voice* (Ongyoku Kowadashi Kuden).

1420   Zeami wrote *On Attainment of the Flower* (Shika Dosho).

1421   Zeami wrote *Diagrams on Song, Dance, and Mime* (Nikyoku Santai Ningyo Zu). Zoami gave a series of subscription Dengaku performances during the Gion Festival.

1422   Zeami became a priest and began dictating his writings to his son Motoyoshi. Motomasa became the third head of the Kanze troupe.

1423   Zeami dictated *On the Composition of Noh Scripts* (No Sakusho) to Motoyoshi. Yoshimochi passed the shogunate on to Yoshikazu, who died only two years later.

1424   Zeami became the master of ceremonies (*gakuto*) for the Daigo Kiyotaki Shrine. He dictated *The Flower Mirror* (Kakyo) and *Five Sounds* (Go-on) to Motoyoshi.

1427   Motoshige performed subscription Noh. The shogun Yoshinori gave his complete patronage to Motoshige from this time on and absolutely ignored Zeami.

1428   Zeami wrote *On Gaining the Jewel and the Flower* (Jugyoku Tokka), which he presented to Komparu Ujinobu (Zenchiku). Former Shogun Yoshimochi died.

1429   Shogun Yoshinori forbade Zeami and his son to ever perform at the retired emperor's palace again. Kanze Masamori was born.

1430   The position of master of ceremonies (*gakuto*) for the Daigo Kiyotaki Shrine was taken from Zeami and given to Motoshige by the shogun. Motoyoshi retired from the stage, and Zeami dictated *Lectures on Sarugaku* to him.

1432   Motomasa died in Ise, and Zeami wrote *A Note After the Dream Has Faded* (Yume no Ato Shisshi) in his memory.

1433   Zeami wrote *The Return of the Flower* (Kyakuraige). Motoshige became fourth head of the Kanze troupe and performed a three-day series of subscription Sarugaku which was attended by Shogun Yoshinori.

1434   Zeami was exiled to Sado.

1436	Zeami wrote *On the Golden Island* (Kintosho).
1443	Zeami died, probably on August 8.
1449	Yoshimasa became shogun.
1450	Subscription Sarugaku was forbidden by the shogun.
1455	Zenchiku wrote *Go-on Shidai*.
1456	Zenchiku wrote *Go-on Jittei, Kabu Zuinoki*, and *Rikurin Ichiro*.
1458	Motoshige became a priest and took the name On'ami. Masamori became the fifth head of the Kanze troupe. Zenchiku wrote his last work, *Emman Iza Hoshiki*, and probably died during this year.
1470	Masamori died at the age of forty-one, and Yukishige took over the Kanze troupe.
1477	The Onin Rebellion ended.
1480	The head of the Komparu troupe, Soin, died at the age of forty-eight.
1481	Kanze Motohiro was born.
1482	Shogun Yoshimasa built the Silver Pavilion (Ginkaku-ji).
1490	Te-sarugaku (Sarugaku performed by amateurs) became popular about this time. Yoshimasa died at the age of fifty-four.
1500	Kanze Yukishige died about this time, and Motohiro took over the Kanze troupe.
1505	Komparu Zempo presented a series of subscription Sarugaku at Awataguchi in Kyoto.
1512	Zempo began writing his *Talks with Zempo* (Zempo Zodan), which he took seven years to complete. About this time, Kanze and Komparu *utai-bon* began to appear for the purpose of teaching *utai* to amateurs.
1516	Kanze Kojiro Nobumitsu died at the age of eighty-one.
1522	Kanze Doken died at the age of forty-four.
1532	Komparu Zempo died at the age of seventy-eight.
1541	Kanze Yajiro died at the age of fifty-three.
1552	*Furyu* dances had been popular in Nara and Kyoto for the last one hundred years.
1555	Komparu Sotan died at the age of seventy-four.
1558	Hosho Ikkan died (age unknown).
1564	Kongo Magojiro Hisatsugu died at the age of twenty-six.
1566	Motohisa became head of the Kanze troupe. Kanze Kokusetsu was born.
1571	Kanze Sosetsu and Motohisa moved their troupe to Hamamatsu, Tokugawa Ieyasu's headquarters.
1572	Hosho Shigekatsu died (age unknown). Damasks and gold brocades became popular for dance costumes in Kyoto.

1573	The Muromachi (Ashikaga) shogunate fell.
1574	Kanze Motoyori died at the age of fifty-five.
1576	Kongo Ujimasa died at the age of sixty-nine. Oda Nobunaga built Azuchi Castle.
1577	Kanze Motohisa died at the age of forty-one.
1578	Sosetsu began to make copies of Zeami's writings about this time.
1582	Te-sarugaku troupes, including those called Horiike and Shibuya, were active about this time. Chinese weaving methods were imported, and gold brocades and damasks were produced in large quantities. Oda Nobunaga died at the age of forty-eight.
1583	Sosetsu died at the age of seventy-four. Hideyoshi built Osaka Castle.
1585	Hideyoshi became *kampaku* (chief adviser to the emperor) and attended a performance of Sarugaku Noh with the emperor.
1586	Kita Shichidayu Nagayoshi was born. Hideyoshi changed his family name to Toyotomi.
1587	Hideyoshi built his mansion Jurakudai.
1588	Gekan Shoshin began to write his *No no Tomecho*.
1592	The four Sarugaku troupes were called to Nagoya in Kyushu by Hideyoshi.
1593	Hideyoshi awarded the mask carver Tsuno-no-bo the red seal proclaiming him "best in the world." Hideyoshi presented Noh in the imperial palace grounds with himself as a performer.
1594	Hideyoshi went flower viewing in Yoshino and made a pilgrimage to Mount Koya, after which he commissioned the writing of two new Noh plays, *Yoshino Hanami* and *Koya Sankei,* and performed the *shite* role in both at his Osaka Castle.
1595	Hideyoshi awarded mask carver Zekan the red seal, proclaiming him "best in the world."
1596	Gekan Shoshin wrote *Dobu Sho.* Hideyoshi performed Noh at Fushimi Castle.
1598	Hideyoshi died at the age of sixty-two.
1600	Kokusetsu performed Noh at Hideyoshi's Jurakudai. About this time Torikai Soseki published the Komparu *utai-bon* entitled *Kurumaya-bon.* Tokugawa Ieyasu defeated Ishida Mitsunari (Hideyoshi's top general and head of the government after Hideyoshi's death) at the battle of Sekigahara.
1603	Tokugawa Ieyasu presented a program of Noh in celebration of his becoming shogun. Okuni from Izumo performed her new Kabuki dances in Kyoto for the first time, thus beginning the development of what we know today as Kabuki.

1604   *Furyu* dances were performed at the Toyokuni Shrine on the anniversary of Hideyoshi's death. All four Noh troupes performed *Okina* as well as new pieces especially written for this occasion. A female Sarugaku troupe was popular in Kyoto at this time.

1609   The four troupes came under the complete control and support of Tokugawa Ieyasu.

1610   Komparu Ujikatsu died at the age of thirty-four. Kongo Katsuyoshi died at the age of forty-eight.

1616   Gekan Shoshin died. Tokugawa Ieyasu died at the age of seventy-four.

1618   The Kita school officially came into being about this time.

1620   Kanze Bokan published the *utai-bon* called *Ganwa Uzuki-bon*.

1621   Komparu Zenkyoku died at the age of seventy-two.

1623   In celebration of becoming shogun, Iemitsu presented a program of Noh in which all four troupes appeared.

1626   Kanze Kokusetsu died at the age of sixty.

1628   The *utai-bon* called *Kan'ei Tamaya-bon* was published.

1630   Hosho Tadakatsu died at the age of seventy-two.

1634   Kita Shichidayu was highly criticized and severely punished for performing at the imperial palace in *Sekidera Komachi,* a piece meant to be performed by no one but the headmasters of the four schools.

1646   The book entitled *A Catalogue of the Actors of the Four Troupes* (Shiza Yakusha Mokuroku) was published.

1647   Noh actors were reprimanded by the shogunate for their officious attitude.

1653   Kita Shichidayu died at the age of sixty-seven.

1658   A book on the choreography of the Kita school entitled *Shichidayu Shimai Tsuke* was published.

1673   *Su utai* became very popular about this time.

1681   The Komparu *utai-bon* entitled *Rokutoku-bon* was published. It contained the librettos for one hundred plays.

1682   Red seals presented to mask carvers by Hideyoshi were declared no longer valid.

1686   An additional one hundred librettos were published as a supplement to the *Rokutoku-bon*.

1687   Books entitled *No no Kummo Zui* and *Nogaku Taizen* were published.

1697   The book entitled *No no Zushiki* was published.

1699   The book entitled *Bugaku Zuiyo Taizen* was published.

1702   Kanze Shigeaki performed a series of subscription Noh at Shichihommatsu in Kyoto.

1716   Kanze Shigenori died at the age of fifty. Yoshimune became shogun.
1728   Hosho Tomoharu died at the age of seventy-four.
1730   Hosho Choei died (age unknown).
1746   Kanze Shigenori died at the age of eighty-nine.
1747   Kanze Kiyochika died at the age of fifty-four.
1750   Kanze Motoaki performed a series of subscription Noh.
1751   Shogun Yoshimune died at the age of sixty-seven.
1752   Kanze Motoaki's younger brother Kiyohisa broke away and formed the Tetsunojo branch of the Kanze school.
1765   The *utai-bon* entitled *Meiwa Kaisei Utai-bon* was published.
1771   The book entitled *Shoka Men Mokuroku* was published.
1772   Kanze Motoaki published *Shudo Sho*. Hosho Tomokiyo died at the age of about sixteen.
1774   Kanze Motoaki died at the age of fifty-two.
1776   The first *utai-bon* of the Kita school was published.
1778   Komparu Ujitsuna died at the age of seventy-one.
1782   Kanze Kiyohisa died at the age of fifty-five.
1791   Hosho Tomokatsu died (age unknown).
1797   Books including *Kamen-fu, Men Mokuri Sho, Jufukusho,* and *Akuma-barai* were published.
1798   The Hosho school published an *utai-bon* for the first time.
1804   Kongo Ujitada died at the age of sixty-nine.
1812   Hosho Hidekatsu died (age unknown).
1815   Kanze Kiyofusa died at the age of fifty-four.
1829   Kita Kono died at the age of eighty-seven.
1841   Noh actors were warned about their behavior by the government.
1848   Subscription Noh was performed by the Hosho school. This was the last performance in history of subscription Noh.
1858   Iemochi became shogun and presented a program of Noh in cele-bration. This was the last performance in celebration of a shogun's taking office.
1863   Hosho Yukan died at the age of sixty-four.
1868   The Meiji Restoration took place.
1869   Kanze Kiyotaka took his troupe to Shizuoka.
1871   Umewaka Minoru I gained possession of the Noh theater at Aoya-ma in Tokyo. Iwakura Tomomi went to Europe.
1874   Kanze Kiyotaka brought his troupe back to Tokyo.
1876   Iwakura returned from Europe and presented a performance of Noh at his own mansion for Emperor Meiji. Umewaka Minoru I, Kanze Tetsunojo I, and Hosho Kuro I appeared in this program.

1878　　A Noh stage was built in the Aoyama Imperial Palace, and Kiyotaka, Kuro, Minoru, Tetsunojo, Komparu Hironari, and Kongo Yuitsu performed there under order of the emperor.

1881　　The Shiba Noh Theater was built, and the organization called the Nogaku-sha was set up.

1882　　The first *utai-bon* of the Kongo school was published.

1884　　Kongo Yuitsu died at the age of sixty-nine.

1888　　Kanze Kiyotaka died at the age of fifty-one.

1896　　A new organization called the Nogaku-kai was set up. Komparu Hironari died at the age of sixty-seven.

1909　　Umewaka Minoru I died at the age of eighty-one. All the works of Zeami were published under the title *Zeami Jurokubu-shu*. Serious research and study of Noh became popular about this time.

1915　　The works of Komparu Zenchiku were published for the first time, greatly facilitating research concerning the Komparu school.

1917　　Hosho Kuro died at the age of eighty. Sakurama Bamba died at the age of eighty-one.

Commentaries on the Illustrations

1. God mask used in the Gion Festival in Kyoto.

2. Goto Tokuzo (foreground) as the ghost of Kiyotsune *(shite)* in *Kiyotsune*. The ghost and his living wife (right) grieve over Kiyotsune's sad death. Part of the chorus is seen at left rear.

3. Kanze Hisao as the god of thunder *(shite)* in *Kamo*. The god of thunder dances and invokes a blessing on the land.

4. Kimura Nobuyuki as the mother *(shite)* in *Sumida-gawa*. The mother prays at the tomb of her son, whom she has been frantically seeking as she wanders about the country.

5. Kanze Motomasa as the angel *(shite)* in *Hagoromo*. The angel dances in gratitude after the fisherman returns her robe of feathers.

6. Kata Minoru (left) as the ghost of Taira Tomomori *(shite)* in *Funa Benkei*. A storm arises and the ghost of Taira Tomomori appears as Minamoto Yoshitsune and his faithful retainer Benkei (right) are crossing an inlet in a boat. A fight ensues, and the ghost is subdued.

7. Umewaka Masatoshi (left center) as the princess *(shite)* in *Momiji-gari*, accompanied by ladies-in-waiting. A demon disguised as a princess entertains Taira Koreshige when he goes to the mountains to view the autumn maple leaves.

8. *Atsuita* costume of heavy brocade decorated with dragons and stylized clouds. Owned by Kongo Iwao, Kyoto.

9. Umewaka Manzaburo as the god of Sumiyoshi *(shite)* in *Takasago*. The god appears as an old man raking fallen leaves.

10. Kita Setsuya as the ghost of Minamoto Yoshitsune *(shite)* in *Yashima*. The ghost of Yoshitsune appears to a traveling priest at Yashima and tells him of the famous battle fought there.

11. Yoshida Nagahiro as the ghost of Taira Tadanori *(shite)* in *Shunzei Tadanori*. Fujiwara Shunzei killed Taira Tadanori in battle. Years later, the ghost of Tadanori appears before Shunzei and requests prayers for the repose of his soul.

12. Kanze Motomasa as the ghost

241

of Ki no Aritsune's daughter *(shite)* in *Izutsu.* The ghost appears to a traveling priest at the Arihara Temple and dances, telling him of her great love for the poet Arihara Narihira, in whose memory the temple was built. As she dances, she wears Narihira's hat and cloak. At right, in front of the chorus, is the well into which she later looks and sees the face of her dead lover.

13. Awaya Kikuo as Yuya *(shite)* in *Yuya.* Yuya weeps as she reads a letter telling of her mother's serious illness. Yuya's patron has forced her to accompany him on a flower-viewing excursion but finally relents and allows her to go to her ailing mother.

14. Kanze Motomasa as the ghost of Lady Naishinno *(shite)* in *Teika.* The ghost appears before a traveling priest and dances, singing of her love for the poet Fujiwara Teika.

15. Kongo Iwao as Jinen Koji *(shite)* in *Jinen Koji.* With a drum tied to his waist, the young priest Jinen Koji dances to gain freedom for a little girl who is in the possession of a slave trader.

16. Umewaka Rokuro as Benkei *(shite)* in *Ataka.* Benkei dances and leaps for joy after he has successfully brought his young master Yoshitsune through the barrier at Ataka.

17. Takagi Koichi as the ghost of the fantastic night bird *(shite)* in *Nue.* The ghost appears before a traveling priest and pleads for prayers for the repose of his soul.

18. Taneda Michio as the demon *(shite)* in *Dojo-ji.* A beautiful dancer's passion for a young priest changes her into a demon serpent.

19. Kita Minoru (left) as the ghost of Fukakusa *(shite)* in *Kayoi Komachi.* The ghosts of Fukakusa and the poetess Komachi *(tsure)* appear before a priest and tell of Fukakusa's great love for Komachi.

20. Honda Hideo as the ghost of a young fisherman *(shite)* in *Fujito.* The ghost appears to the warrior Sasaki Moritsuna and expresses gratitude for prayers for his soul.

21. Shimazawa Keijiro as Emma, king of hell *(shite),* in *Ukai.* Emma appears before a traveling priest and asks him to pray for the soul of a cormorant fisherman who is in hell because he spent his life destroying the lives of fish.

22. Kondo Kenzo as Komachi *(shite)* in *Sotoba Komachi.* A traveling priest meets the formerly beautiful poetess Komachi, who has now become a penniless old woman. She tells him of her difficult present life and recalls the days of her youth.

23. Kongo Iwao as the dragon god *(shite)* in *Kasuga Ryujin.* The dragon god appears and dances for the head priest of the Kasuga Shrine at Nara.

24. Taue no Dengaku (Dengaku rice-planting dance). Detail from a a folding screen depicting medieval manners and customs. Tokyo National Museum.

25. Dancers wearing Noh masks. Detail from a folding screen called *Toyokuni Sairei Zu Byobu* (Screen Picturing Scenes from the Toyokuni Festival). Owned by the Tokugawa Reimeikai, Tokyo.

26. Kanze Noh. Detail from a folding screen called *Rakuchu Rakugai Zu Byobu* (Screen Picturing Scenes in and Around Kyoto). Owned by Machida Manjiro, Tokyo.

27. Noh stage for the Toyokuni Festival, Kyoto. Detail from a folding screen called *Toyokuni Sairei Zu Byobu* (Screen Picturing Scenes from the Toyokuni Festival). Owned by the Tokugawa Reimeikai, Tokyo.

28–29. Illustrated *utai-bon* of the Noh play *Hyakuman*. Probably painted around the beginning of the eighteenth century during the Genroku era (1688–1703). Owned by Ikuta Shinzo, Kyoto.

30. Jo mask carved in 1430. Owned by the Amagawa Benzaiten Shrine, Yoshino County, Nara Prefecture.

31. Sections of a bow with drawings of Sangaku performers. Eighth century. Shoso-in, Nara.

32–33. Details from *Shinzai Kogaku Zu* showing various forms of Sangaku during the Heian period (794–1185). Owned by the Tokyo University of Fine Arts.

34–35. Dengaku performed at a festival (34) and in front of the gate of a nobleman's residence (35). Details from *Nenju Gyoji Emaki*, a scroll

picturing annual court functions during the late Heian period (eleventh to twelfth century). Owned by Tanaka Shimbi, Tokyo.

36. Heian-period (794–1185) dance called *gosechi-no-mai*. Detail from a folding screen known as *Tomoyoshi Zu Byobu* (Screen Picturing Scenes at Tomoyoshi). Owned by Yabumoto Soshiro, Tokyo.

37. Dance called *gosechi-no-mai*. Detail from *Nenju Gyoji Emaki*, a scroll picturing annual court functions during the late Heian period (eleventh to twelfth century). Owned by Tanaka Shimbi, Tokyo.

38. *Shirabyoshi* dancer (right) and *kuse-mai* dancer (left). Detail from *Nanajuichiban Shokunin Uta-awase*, a medieval collection of illustrated poems. Owned by Haneishi Koji, Tokyo.

39. Performance of the medieval popular-song genre called *imayo*. Detail from the fourteenth-century picture scroll known as *Kasuga Gongen Reigenki Emaki*. Owned by the Imperial Household Agency, Tokyo.

40. Gourd-beater *(hachi-tataki)* priest (left) and juggler *(hoka)* priest who provided chanted and rhythmical accompaniment to lively popular dances. Detail from *Nanajuichiban Shokunin Uta-awase*, a medieval collection of illustrated poems. Owned by Haneishi Koji, Tokyo.

41: Man performing sword tricks. Detail from a painting on a paper door *(fusuma-e)* in Nagoya Castle. Momoyama period (1573–1602).

42. Chichi-no-jo mask. Owned by Kamikado Shiro, Fukui Prefecture.

43. Okina mask. Owned by Mitsui Hachiroemon, Tokyo.

44. *Rambu* (mime-type Sarugaku with song and dance elements). Detail from the sixteenth-century picture scroll *Ashibiki Emaki*. Owned by the Itsuo Art Museum, Osaka.

45. Medieval form of dramatic recitation known as *etoki*. Detail from a folding screen depicting scenes in and around Kyoto. Owned by Wakimura Yoshitaro, Zushi, Kanagawa Prefecture.

46. Two pages from libretto for medieval dramatic form called *enkyoku*. Owned by the Japanese Language Research Department, Kyoto University.

47. Sarugaku (left) and Dengaku (right) dancers. Detail from a sixteenth-century picture scroll known as *Tsurugaoka Hosho-e Shokunin Utaawase Emaki*. Owned by Matsushita Konosuke, Nishinomiya, Hyogo Prefecture.

48. Sambaso mask. Owned by the Hiyoshi Shrine, Otsu, Shiga Prefecture.

49. Demon mask. Owned by the Ibuki Shrine, Nagahama, Shiga Prefecture.

50, 51. Two types of sacred Noh performed at the Wakamiya Festival of the Kasuga Shrine at Nara. 50: *otabisho* Noh: performance of Noh at one of the resting places of the portable shrine. 51: *takigi* (firelight) Noh. Details from the medieval picture scroll *Wakamiya Sairei Emaki*. Owned by the Kasuga Shrine, Nara.

52. Donation list of the Hogen Temple in Nara which records a gift of land from Zeami.

53. Portrait statue of Ashikaga Yoshimitsu. Owned by the Toji-in, Kyoto.

54. Document written in Zeami's hand. Owned by the Hozan-ji, Ikoma County, Nara Prefecture.

55. Detail from libretto of the Noh play *Eguchi* written in Zeami's hand. Owned by the Hozan-ji, Ikoma County, Nara Prefecture.

56. Pages from Zeami's *Fushi Kaden* (The Transmission of the Flower of the Art), better known as the *Kadensho*. Owned by Kanze Motomasa, Tokyo.

57, 58. Details from Zeami's *Diagrams on Song, Dance, and Mime* (Nikyoku Santai Ningyo Zu). Owned by Kanze Motomasa, Tokyo.

59, 60. Last page (left) and front cover (right) of *utai-bon* written by Zempo. Owned by the Noh Research Center, Hosei University, Tokyo.

61, 62. Last page (left) and front cover (right) of *utai-bon* written by Kojiro Motoyori. Owned by the Noh Research Center, Hosei University, Tokyo.

63. Page from Zenchiku's *Six Blossoms and One Drop of Dew* (Rikurin

Ichiro). Owned by Komparu Nobutaka, Tokyo.

64. Floor plan of stage and seating arrangement of patrons for a subscription Noh performance in 1464. Owned by Kanze Motomasa, Tokyo.

65. Fudo mask. Owned by Mitsui Hachiroemon, Tokyo.

66. Aku-no-jo mask. Owned by the Oyama Shrine, Kanazawa, Ishikawa Prefecture.

67. Portrait of Kita Shichidayu. Owned by Kita Minoru, Tokyo.

68. Two pages from Gekan Shoshin's *Dobu Sho*. Owned by Ejima Iemon, Tokyo.

69. Record of stipends paid by Hideyoshi to actors of the Kanze troupe. Owned by Kanze Motomasa, Tokyo.

70. Record of stipends paid by Hideyoshi to actors of the Kongo troupe. Owned by Mitsui Hachiroemon, Tokyo.

71. Detail from libretto of the Noh play *Matsukaze* with choreography by Motoaki. Owned by Kanze Motomasa, Tokyo.

72, 73. Sample page (left) and front cover (right) of *A Catalogue of Noh Masks* (Shoka Men Mokuroku), published in 1771. Owned by Kanze Motomasa, Tokyo.

74. *Utai* teacher. Detail from the medieval picture scroll *Kabuki Zumaki*. Owned by the Tokugawa Reimeikai, Tokyo.

75. Drawing of inside of a theater built for an eighteenth-century performance of subscription Noh by the Hosho troupe. Owned by the Noh Research center, Hosei University, Tokyo.

76. Edo-period (1603–1868) painting of a performance of Noh for the common people (*machi-iri* Noh). Owned by the Noh Research Center of Hosei University, Tokyo.

77. Mask carver. Detail from an Edo-period (1603–1868) book, *Jinrin Kummo Zui*, dealing with contemporary occupations.

78. Yase-otoko mask, used for aged male roles. Owned by Mitsui Hachiroemon, Tokyo.

79. Magojiro mask, used for young female roles. Owned by Mitsui Hachiroemon, Tokyo.

80. Chujo mask, used for warrior-ghost roles. Owned by Mitsui Hachiroemon, Tokyo.

81. Cloaklike costume called *choken*. Owned by Kongo Iwao, Kyoto.

82. Gold-brocade costume called *karaori*. Owned by Kongo Iwao, Kyoto.

83. Musical instruments used in Noh. Lower left: *kotsuzumi* (small hand drum) with drumheads detached. Center left: *otsuzumi* (large hand drum). Upper right: *taiko* (floor drum). Lower right: *fue* (flute).

84. Noh fans called *ogi*. Top center: *shura* (warrior-ghost) *ogi*. Upper left: *kami* (god) *ogi*. Upper right: *katsura*

(wig or woman) *ogi*. Center left: *rojo* (old woman) *ogi*. Center right: *oni* (demon) *ogi*. Lower left: *doji* (young boy) *ogi*. Lower right: *otoko* (man) *ogi*. Owned by Katayama Hirotaro, Kyoto.

85. The Tokyo mask carver Irie Miho putting the final touches of color on a new Noh mask.

86. Kanze Motomasa, headmaster of the Kanze school, in rehearsal.

87. Kanze Motomasa teaching at the Tokyo University of Fine Arts.

88. Kanze Motomasa teaching his students at the Kanze Noh Theater in Tokyo.

89. Kanze Motomasa teaching his own son.

90. Kanze Motomasa conducting a rehearsal at the Kanze Noh Theater in Tokyo.

91. Kanze Motomasa studying the writings of his predecessors.

92. Shiwa-jo mask, used for aged male roles. Owned by Kanze Motomasa, Tokyo.

93. Sho-jo mask, used for aged male roles. Owned by Mitsui Hachiroemon, Tokyo.

94. Heida mask, used for warrior-ghost roles. Owned by Kongo Iwao, Kyoto.

95. Kaishi mask, used for ghost roles. Owned by Mitsui Hachiroemon, Tokyo.

96. Otobide mask, used for demon roles. Owned by Kongo Iwao, Kyoto.

97. Obeshimi mask, used for demon roles. Owned by the Kumano Yasumi Shrine, Toyohashi, Aichi Prefecture.

98. Zo-onna mask, used for roles of beautiful middle-aged women. Owned by Hosho Kuro, Tokyo.

99. Ko-omote mask, used for roles of beautiful young women. Owned by Kongo Iwao, Kyoto.

100. Yase-onna mask, used for middle-aged female roles. Owned by Mitsui Hachiroemon, Tokyo.

101. Kasshiki mask, used for roles of handsome young men. Owned by Kanze Motomasa, Tokyo.

102. Shintai mask, used for god roles. Owned by the Taga Shrine, Inukami County, Shiga Prefecture.

103. Imawaka mask, used for young male roles. Owned by Kanze Motomasa, Tokyo.

104. Shunkan mask, used only for the role of Shunkan. Owned by Kanze Motomasa, Tokyo.

105. Hannya mask, used for ghosts of jealous women. Owned by Kongo Iwao, Kyoto.

106. Shikami mask, used for roles of angry ghosts. Owned by Mitsui Hachiroemon, Tokyo.

107. Shishi-guchi mask, used for

lion roles. Owned by Kanze Moto-masa, Tokyo.

108. Brocade costume called *karaori*. Owned by Kanze Tetsunojo, Tokyo.

109. Jacketlike brocade costume called *kariginu*. Owned by Kanze Motomasa, Tokyo.

110. Cloaklike garment called *suo*. Owned by Kongo Iwao, Kyoto.

111. Undergarment called *surihaku*. Owned by the Seki Kasuga Shrine, Seki, Gifu Prefecture.

112. Trouserlike garment called *hangiri*. Owned by Kongo Iwao, Kyoto.

113. Cloaklike garment called *happi*. Owned by Umewaka Rokuro, Tokyo.

114–19. Preparations for a performance of *Hyakuman* by Hosho Kuro, headmaster of the Hosho school.

114. Putting on the *surihaku* under-garment.

115. The *nuihaku* outer garment is bound around the hips in *koshimaki* style.

116. The actor salutes the mask before placing it over his face.

117. The actor contemplates his appearance in the greenroom *(kagami-no-ma)* while awaiting his cue.

118. The actor passes under the upraised curtain and onto the *hashigakari*, which leads to the stage proper.

119. The actor arrives on the stage proper.

120. Modern Noh stage in the Kanze Noh Theater, Tokyo.

121. Sixteenth-century Noh stage at the Nishi Hongan-ji, Kyoto.

122–35. Various stage properties shown in the plays in which they are used.

122. Thatched hut: *Semimaru*.

123. Shrine: *Yokihi*.

124. Mountain: *Momiji-gari*.

125. Thatched hut: *Kagekiyo*.

126. Prison: *Rodaiko*.

127. Palanquin: *Nonomiya*.

128. Boat: *Eguchi*.

129. Bell tower: *Mii-dera*.

130. Salt-gathering cart: *Matsukaze*.

131. Fulling block: *Kinuta*.

132. Bell: *Dojo-ji*.

133. Drum stand. *Tenko*.

134. Yoke and water buckets: *Genjo*.

135. Spinning wheel: *Kurozuka*.

136–43. Various *kata* (movement patterns) demonstrated by Kongo Iwao, headmaster of the Kongo school.

136. *Kane-no-ogi*. The fan is held in a vertical position parallel to the body, indicating the act of listening.

137. *Tsuki-no-ogi*. The fan is held vertically near the shoulder, the eyes raised to look into the distance, usually indicating the act of viewing the moon.

138, 139. Two forms of *hane-ogi,* a *kata* which usually indicates the act of viewing flowers. In the first (138) the fan is held at an oblique angle in front of the forehead. In the second (139) the fan is held in a vertical position in front of the chest, the eyes slightly lowered.

140. *Shikake.* The fan is lifted from the side to an almost horizontal position in front of the chest. A dance movement.

141. *Hiraki.* The fan is moved from the position in Plate 140 to a raised horizontal position at the side. A dance movement.

142. *Makura-no-ogi.* The fan is held in front of the face, the body in a kneeling position and the head inclined forward, usually indicating sleep.

143. *Agehane.* The fan is raised from the side to a vertical position in front of the chest. A dance movement.

144–51. Various *kata* (movement patterns) demonstrated by Komparu Nobutaka.

144. *Kamae.* The basic pose.

145. *Gassho.* With the body in a kneeling position, the tips of the fingers touch in front of the chest to indicate prayer or a plea.

146. *Ashi-byoshi.* The strong beat of the feet. The foot is lifted straight up and lowered forcefully.

147. *Hakobi.* The movement of the feet in walking. The heels never leave the floor.

148. *Ryo-shiori.* With the body in a seated position, both hands are lifted to a position in front of the eyes to indicate especially deep sorrow.

149. *Kata-shiori.* One handed is lifted in front of the eyes and the head is tilted forward to indicate weeping.

150. *Naginata.* The use of the halberd in describing a battle.

151. *Maki-sode.* The sleeve is flipped up so that it hangs lightly wrapped around the arm. This *kata* is used at the climax of dances expressing great elation.

152, 153. The Tokyo mask carver Irie Miho at work.

154, 155. Weaving cloth for Noh costumes. The weaver is Nakajima Yasojiro, of Kyoto.

156. A Kyoto fanmaker at work. The fans are of the *chukei* type.

157. Putting the final touches to a pair of snow-white *tabi* socks.

158. Festival Noh: a performance of *Ataka* on a temporary stage placed on the stage of a proscenium theater.

159. Scene from *Fukkatsu,* a modern Noh play using the Resurrection as its theme. At left: Kita Minoru.

160. Scene from *Tsuru,* a recently composed Noh play, with Kita Minoru as the *shite.*

161. Scene from *Yuzuru,* a modern play using Noh techniques.

The "weathermark"
identifies this book as having been
planned, designed, and produced at
the Tokyo offices of
John Weatherhill, Inc.
7–6–13 Roppongi, Minato-ku, Tokyo 106
Book design and typography by Ronald V. Bell
Layout of photographs by Tanko-sha, Kyoto
Composition by Samhwa Printing Co., Ltd., Seoul
Color and gravure plates engraved and printed by
Dai Nippon Printing Co., Ltd., Tokyo
Text printed by Kinmei Printing Co., Ltd., Tokyo
Binding by Okamoto Binderies, Tokyo
Set in 11-point Monotype Baskerville
with hand-set Bulmer for display